॥ શ્રી સ્વામિનારાયણો વિજયતેતરામ્ ॥

S S Temple OLDHAM

with compliments
Shree Swaminarayan Temple
270 Lee Street, Oldham, Lancashire, UK, OL8 1BG
Tel/Fax 0161 652 0993 Charity Reg. No. 509271
www.swaminarayan-oldham.org

Life and Faith of

LORD SWAMINARAYAN

S S Temple OLDHAM

Shree Swaminarayan Temple, Oldham, UK

Under Shree NarNarayan Dev Temple, Bhuj, Kutch, India

Life and Faith of Lord Swaminarayan

Published by:

Shree Swaminarayan Temple
270 Lee Street
Oldham
United Kingdom
OL8 1BG

Tel / Fax: 0161 652 0993

Registered Charity Number: 509271

Website: www.swaminarayan-oldham.org
Email: info@swaminarayan-oldham.org

Published 2002

ISBN: 0 9542220 0 8

Printed by: Mankul Industries, Mumbai, India
Website: www.mankul.com

CONTENTS

|| *Shree Swaminarayano Vijaytetram* ||

Jai Shree Swaminarayan

This publication 'Life and Faith of Lord Swaminarayan' describes the greatness of our beloved Lord Swaminarayan and our Swaminarayan Sampraday. The publication coincides with the 25th anniversary of Shree Swaminarayan Temple Oldham.

The young satsangis of Oldham have produced this book with great dedication of time and effort. We hope this book will give fellow satsangis a clear, concise and everlasting insight into our Swaminarayan Sampraday, leaving a permanent mark on their lives.

May Lord Swaminarayan shower His blessings on our anniversary and the future of Shree Swaminarayan Temple Oldham.

Shree Swaminarayan Temple Oldham

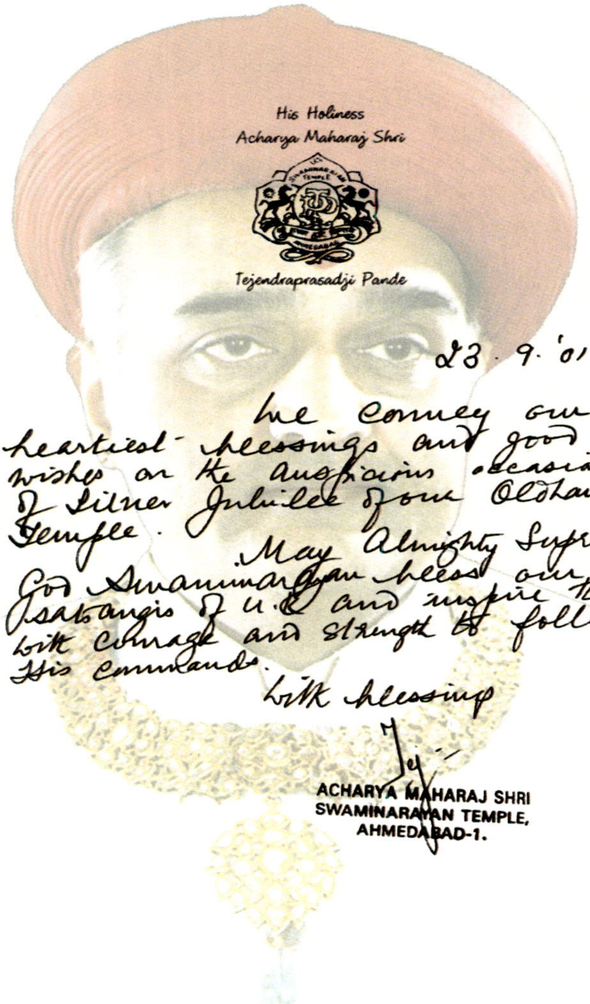

His Holiness
Acharya Maharaj Shri

Tejendraprasadji Pande

23. 9. '01

We convey our heartiest blessings and good wishes on the auspicious occasion of Silver Jubilee of our Oldham Temple.

May Almighty Supreme God Swaminarayan bless our satsangis of U.K and inspire them with courage and strength to follow His commands.

With blessings

Tej

ACHARYA MAHARAJ SHRI
SWAMINARAYAN TEMPLE,
AHMEDABAD-1.

રજી. ટ્રસ્ટ રજીસ્ટર નં. A ૨૩ કચ્છ. ॥ શ્રી સ્વામિનારાયણો વિજયતેતરામ ॥ ☎ ૨૨૩૩૧ ૨૩૩૩૧

SHREE SWAMINARAYAN TEMPLE

SWAMINARAYAN ROAD, POST BHUJ (KUTCH) 370001.

卐 શ્રી સ્વામિનારાયણ મંદિર, ભુજ – કચ્છ. 卐

તારીખ / DATE ૨૭-૧૦-૨૦૦૧

સ્વસ્તિ શ્રી ઓલ્ડહામ મહા શુભ સ્થાને પરમ પવિત્ર શ્રી સહજાનંદ સ્વામીના પરમ ઉપાસક, અને શ્રીજી મહારાજ કૃત ધર્મ મર્યાદા પાલન તત્પર, શ્રીજી મહારાજના પરમ ભક્તિ અને અમારા અનન્ય એવા સત્સંગી શિરોમણી પરમ ભાગવદીય શ્રી સ્વામિનારાયણ મંદિર, ઓલ્ડહામ ના માનનીય પ્રમુખ શ્રી, ઉપ પ્રમુખ શ્રી, મંત્રી શ્રી, સહમંત્રી શ્રી, ખજાનચી શ્રી, કારોબારી કમિટી તથા ટ્રસ્ટી મંડળના સભ્યો તથા નાના મોટા સૌ હરિભક્તો પ્રત્યે...

અત્ર શ્રીમન્ નરનારાયણ દેવના ચરણ કમળ સાન્નિધ્ય શુભસ્થાનથી ભુજથી લિ. મહંત સ્વામી પુરાણી હરિસ્વરૂપદાસજી તથા સ.ગુ. સ્વામી ધર્મકિશોરદાસજી તથા ઉપ. મહંત સ્વામી પુરાણી ધર્મનંદનદાસજી તથા પારસદ સમસ્ત ભગત આદી સંત મંડળના સપ્રેમ જય શ્રી સ્વામિનારાયણ વાંચશો.

આપના મંદિરનો ૨૫ મો વાર્ષિક પાટોત્સવ અને ૨૦૦૨ ના વર્ષમાં ધામધૂમથી ઉજવવા માગો છો. અને પ્રસંગને અનુરૂપ એક સોવિનીયર (પુસ્તીકા) બહાર પાડવા માગો છો તે જાણીને અમોને ખુબ આનંદ થયો છે. આ સોવિનીયર માં ઉપયોગી લેખો, સંસ્થાની ધાર્મિક તેમજ શૈક્ષણિક અને સામાજીક પ્રવૃતિઓ દર્શાવતો વર્તમાન તેમજ ભવિષ્યની પ્રગતિ માટે રાહબર થશે. આપ સર્વે એક જુથ થઈને ભાઈચારો અને સંગઠનની ઊંચી ભાવના રાખીને જે કાર્ય કરી રહ્યા છો તેનાથી ધાર્મિક સંસ્થાઓ અને સામાજીક સંસ્થાઓની ખુબ સારી પ્રગતિ થશે. અને આવા ધાર્મિક ઉત્સવોથી ભાવિ પેઢીના યુવાન હરિભક્તોમાં પણ સારા સંસ્કારનું સિંચન થશે.

આપના ૨૫ માં વાર્ષિક પાટોત્સવની ઉજવણીમાં અને સેવાના કાર્યોમાં જે કોઈએ પણ ભાગ લીધો હશે તેઓનું જરૂરથી કલ્યાણ થશે. અને આપનો આ ભવ્ય કાર્યક્રમ નિરવિઘ્ને પૂર્ણ થાય અને સૌ કાર્યકર હરિભક્તોને શ્રીજી મહારાજ આ કાર્ય માટે શક્તિ આપે એવી અમો શ્રી નરનારાયણ દેવ પાસે પ્રાર્થના કરીએ છીએ. રાજી રહેજો.

અત્રેથી સંત મંડળના સપ્રેમ જય શ્રી સ્વામિનારાયણ વાંચશો.

લિ. પુરાણી ધર્મનંદનદાસજીના સપ્રેમ જય શ્રી સ્વામિનારાયણ વાંચશોજી

" આપના મંદિરનો ૨૫ મો પાટોત્સવસને ૨૦૦૨ ના વર્ષ માં ધામધુમથી ઊજવવા માગો છો, અને પ્રસંગને અનુરૂપ એક સોવિનીયર (પુસ્તીકા) બહાર પાડવા માગો છો, તે જાણીને અમોને ખુબ આનંદ થયો છે. "

" ...આવા સોવિનીયર દ્વારા ભાવિપેઢીના યુવાન હરિભક્તોમાં પણ જરૂર સારા સંસ્કારોનું સિંચન થશે. "

Shree Swaminarayan Temple Oldham

Lord Swaminarayan

Shree Swaminarayan Temple Oldham

Ghanshyam Maharaj

Shree Swaminarayan Temple Oldham

NarNarayan Dev & Radha Krishna
HariKrishna Maharaj

Shree Swaminarayan Temple Oldham

Manaki Ghodi

Sihasan

Shree Swaminarayan Temple Oldham

Hanumanji

Ganapatiji

Aims of writing this book

We have aimed to capture the essence of our beloved Lord Swaminarayan, His life and His teachings in this book. This book has been written to provide guidance and information in the lives of all satsangis.

Within our sampraday there are numerous scriptures and texts readily available in Gujarati. The younger generations of today have limited knowledge of our Swaminarayan Sampraday and find it difficult to acquire knowledge from Gujarati literature. It is for this reason that our sampraday must produce religious texts in English that depict the life and message of Lord Swaminarayan in greater clarity.

We set ourselves this difficult task of writing a religious book that would have its own permanent place on the bookshelf of every satsangi. There were many a time when the project seemed too onerous for the younger generation writing the book, but with the strength and blessings of Lord Swaminarayan we continued and have completed our goal.

Shree Swaminarayan Temple Oldham has published this book, providing knowledge on a wide range of areas, hoping that it will act as a lasting reference book for the youngsters in the UK and abroad.

Our Sampraday

The Swaminarayan Sampraday has grown strongly under the guidance of the Acharya Maharaj Shri, respected saints and elders. Over a short period of time the message of Lord Swaminarayan has spread to all corners of the world.

The respected saints guided our ancestors in their lives and in their migration from east to west. Our ancestors suffered great hardships to secure a comfortable and prosperous life for the future generations, for which we will be eternally grateful. They did this with complete single-minded faith and trust in Lord Swaminarayan. Today, we reap the rewards of their courage and efforts.

We have a unique sampraday that should be lovingly embraced, maintaining our tradition and always being aware of our identity. Our ancestors have laid down solid foundations for the sampraday, by having strong devotion and belief in Lord Swaminarayan.

As with all walks of life there are difficulties and obstacles in religion too, these must always be viewed as challenges. By leading a moral life, with the blessings of Lord Swaminarayan, we shall emerge together, with a stronger belief in Almighty God Supreme.

History of Shree Swaminarayan Temple Oldham

Religion and belief in God was a key part of the satsangis that settled in Oldham. Originally, religious sabhas were held at the Music Hall in Werneth Park as satsangi numbers grew to nearly 500. The Late Mahant Swami of Bhuj, Shastri Swami Dharmajeevandasji often sent prasad to satsangis in Oldham from India, which was then distributed within the community.

Acharya Maharaj Shri Tejendraprasadji visited Oldham in 1976 and suggested that we should build a temple in Oldham and firmly establish the Swaminarayan satsang in Oldham.

Acharya Maharaj Shri presented a divine murti of Lord Swaminarayan to the satsangis of Oldham. This very same murti of Lord Swaminarayan is residing in the centre of our temple sinhasan today.

With the blessings of His Holiness Acharya Maharaj Shri Tejendraprasadji and the Late Mahant Shastri Swami Dharmajeevandasji and other great saints of Bhuj Mandir, a Baptist Church on Lee Street was bought in June 1977. It was so derelict that everything was stripped to the bricks and then renovated. All the satsangis, including children,

worked day and night to have the temple completed for an official opening before Diwali of that year. With all the time and effort put in by the satsangis, the temple was completed well before Diwali. The official opening was on 22nd October 1977.

Oldham temple was the third Swaminarayan temple in the UK. It was the first Swaminarayan temple to hold prayer services 7 days a week both mornings and evenings. The temple has been open for darshan every single day since the opening

The elders were keen to maintain the mother tongue Gujarati alive amongst the youngsters. Therefore, a Sunday Gujarati school was formed when the temple opened. This school was the first to be established amongst the Swaminarayan temples of England. The first classes commenced in November 1977.

In 1978, the temple Sports Club was formed to encourage youngsters to attend temple and play their part in the satsang. There were originally 40 members, some of whom are members even to this day.

In October 1980, a new altar was shipped from India and installed in the temple. The altar weighed a staggering two tonnes, costing £4,000 and standing 16ft high. It is hand carved out of teak and took 40 satsangis one week to put together. It was one of the first of its kind in Britain.

Kanbis journey from India

In the early 1900s, prospects and employment in Kutch were poor. As a result, the Kanbi communities in Kutch struggled and times were hard.

Opportunities were identified in East Africa and many Indians were leaving India to work in Africa. Respected Head Saints of Bhuj Mandir, Sadguru Swami Shreevallabhdasji and Sadguru Swami Nilkanthdasji, along with elder members of the community urged satsangis to go to East Africa for their future and well being of their families.

Thousands of Kanbis left the villages of Kutch and went to countries like Kenya, Uganda and Tanzania for work. The ambitious and hard working Kanbis quickly settled into life and prospered.

In the latter half of the 20th Century, Kanbis were well established in the British colonies of East Africa. Having resided in East Africa for several years, they had the right to become British citizens. Many grasped this opportunity and secured their future. This enabled the Kanbis who had settled in East Africa to migrate to the United Kingdom.

Kanbis arrival to Oldham

The first Kanbis came and settled in Oldham in 1965. The level of education was basic. Oldham was the global centre of the cotton and textile industry. The cotton mills in the area offered many job opportunities. The jobs were secure, indoor and provided a steady income.

Over a short period of time, the Kanbi community became strong as more and more people arrived into the town.

In the past the Kanbi community has gone through years of difficulty in India and East Africa. As a result of the vision and direction of great saints we are now all very well placed in society. Kanbis have excelled in various walks of life through education, hard work and dedication.

Manifestation of God

Lord Shree Krishna said to Arjun...

> *"When evil dominates good, and righteous people are suffering, Lord Almighty incarnates Himself on earth in human form"*
>
> *(Shreemad Bhagwad Gita)*
>
> यदा यदा हि धर्मस्य ग्लानिर्भवति भारत,
> अभ्युत्थानम धर्मस्य तदात्मानं सृजाम्यहम् ।
> परित्राणाय साधुनां विनाशाय च दुष्कृताम,
> धर्मसंस्थापनार्थाय संभवामि युगे युगे ॥

Lord NarNarayan had gathered in Badrikashram, a place of Gods. The gathering was awaiting news from Rishis who had visited Bharatkhund to determine the status of life and social conditions. Uddhavji, Murti, Dharma and other Rishis were present in the sabha.

On arrival of the Rishis from Bharat, Lord NarNarayan and other members of the sabha were in deep conversation discussing the findings of the Rishis.

Durvasha Muni arrived at the sabha from Mount Kailash. On his entry to the sabha nobody acknowledged him, as they were all in deep discussion. As a result, Durvasha Muni felt humiliated. He was renowned for his bursts of anger and short temper, and thereby cursed all the members that were present to be born once again on Earth.

Gathering in Badrikashram

Everyone was shocked by the wrath of Durvasha Muni. Reassuringly Lord NarNarayan explained to all those present that the curse was His wish, as He Himself would descend onto earth to destroy evil and to establish good moral codes.

Lord Swaminarayan's parents

Dharmadev was the Lord's father and Bhaktimata was His mother. The parents of Lord Swaminarayan took birth on earth due to the curse of Durvasha Muni in Badrikashram, where they were known as Dharma and Murti.

The family of Dharmadev was Sarvaria Brahmin by caste and the family surname was Pande. Dharmadev was also known as Hari Prasad Pande and was born in a town called Ittar in Uttar Pradesh. He was very learned and respected by great scholars of the time. Bala Krishna and Bhagyawati were the parents of Dharmadev.

Bhaktimata was also born a Brahmin and was called Baladevi prior to her marriage to Dharmadev. She was born in Chhapaiya. Krishna Sharma and Bhawani Devi were the parents of Bhaktimata.

Through God's wish they were always destined to marry one another, since Lord Narayan wanted to take birth into their family. After their marriage they stayed in Ayodhya. In Ayodhya, demons and evil forces constantly harassed Dharmadev and Bhaktimata. They struggled for food and their lives were made extremely difficult. To free themselves from the difficulties they prayed to Hanuman at Hanuman Gaddhi in Ayodhya.

Hanuman asked Dharmadev and Bhaktimata to go to Vrindavan and do penance of God. Dharmadev and Bhaktimata had complete faith in Hanuman, and therefore went to Vrindavan where all members of the Badrikashram sabha were present. On performing strict penance, Lord Krishna was much pleased and gave divine darshan of Himself to all.

Lord Krishna revealed to Dharmadev and Bhaktimata that He Himself would take birth as their Son and that peace would return to their lives. Dharmadev and Bhaktimata were overjoyed on hearing this, they then started their return journey home.

On their journey home they met the great demon Aswathama, who was the archenemy of Lord Krishna. Ashwathama asked where they had been, Dharmadev and Bhaktimata told him the whole story and that Almighty God Supreme would take birth as their son.

On hearing this, Ashwathama was filled with anger. He immediately cursed Dharmadev and Bhaktimata and said that their Son, Almighty God Supreme, would not take use of weapons to defeat evil forces. Ashwathama had said this since he falsely believed that this would prevent the conquering of demon warriors. Dharmadev and Bhaktimata were extremely saddened, but continued their journey home.

Birth of Lord Swaminarayan

Almighty Lord Swaminarayan took birth on this earth in Chhapaiya (Uttar Pradesh) at 10:10pm on Monday 9th day of the bright half of the month Chaitra VS 1837 (2 April 1781 AD), also the birthday of Lord Ram.

Markendey Muni, a famous astrologer, arrived in Chhapaiya and through the request of the Lord's parents gave Lord Swaminarayan the names of Krishna, Hari, Hari Krishna and Nilkanth. The family of the Lord addressed Him by His pet name of Ghanshyam.

Family of Lord Swaminarayan

Lord Swaminarayan had two brothers. Rampratapji was the eldest and was 19 years older than Lord. Iccharamji was 5 years younger than Lord.

Rampratapji was married to Suvasinibai, had three sons and one daughter named Dhanbai. Nandram was the eldest son and Ayodhyaprasadji (Lord Swaminarayan's adopted son) was second.

Iccharamji was married to Varyadibai. Iccharamji had five sons and two daughters. Their eldest son was Sitaram and Raghuvirji (Lord Swaminarayan's adopted son) was fourth.

Childhood

Ghanshyam spent the initial few years of His childhood in Chhapaiya. In Chhapaiya, Lord was often harassed and troubled by demons and evil forces. His parents, Dharmadev and Bhaktimata therefore decided to move to Ayodhya a few miles away, when Ghanshyam was aged three.

Chaul Sanskar (hair removing ceremony)

Hindu religion dictates that the first hair of a child after birth is sacred. The removal of this hair should be performed under certain ceremonial conditions. Ghanshyam had this ceremony performed at the age of three.

During the ceremony the demon Kalidatta came to Chhapaiya to kill Lord Almighty with his evil forces.

Ghanshyam used His divine powers to kill the demon Kalidatta at that young age.

Khampa Lake

Ghanshyam was very fond of listening to katha from a young age. A sage called Haridas used to read the Ramayan daily at the edge of Khampa Lake in Chhapaiya.

Ghanshyam would go to listen to the katha with His friends. After listening to katha, Ghanshyam with His friends went to bathe in the lake and played in the tamarind (ambli) tree next to the lake.

On one occasion, during the excitement of playing on the tree, Ghanshyam hurt Himself on His right thigh and started to bleed badly. Ashwinikumar, a divine doctor quickly arrived at the lakeside to help Ghanshyam and placed bandages on Ghanshyam's thigh. The wound left a permanent scar on the thigh of Ghanshyam.

Khampa Lake and the area of the tamarind tree are still present in Chhapaiya to this day.

Yagnopavit ceremony (sacred thread)

At the age of 8, the family of Ghanshyam conducted the Janoi ceremony for Lord Almighty.

Yagnopavit ceremony is when a male adorns 3 sacred strands. The 3 strands represent Brahma, Vishnu and Shiva, being the creator, preserver and destroyer respectively.

The ceremony places emphasis on celibacy (Brahmcharya) and moral behaviour. Those who wear the janoi ensure that the sacred thread is never taken off, just as with kanthi.

Throughout childhood Ghanshyam wanted to escape from family life and leave for pilgrimage. On completion of the Janoi ceremony Ghanshyam left home. But His Vishram Mama chased after Him and persuaded Him to stay.

Study of Scriptures (Shastras)

Ghanshyam commenced the studies of the scriptures at the age of five.

Dharmadev, Ghanshyam's father, was a learned scholar and also His personal tutor. Ghanshyam was a divine student with extraordinary learning powers. Ghanshyam would bathe daily in the River Saryu and then attend the religious discourses at the numerous temples in Ayodhya.

Ghanshyam mastered the Vedas by the tender age of 10. From His experience and knowledge He prepared a summary booklet that captured the nectar of all scriptures.

At the age of 10, Ghanshyam accompanied by His parents went for pilgrimage to Kashi (Varanasi), a holy city where many prominent scholars resided. Many great scholars respected Dharmadev in Kashi.

Ghanshyam took part and excelled in many debates and discussions in Kashi with other respected scholars. He proved to the great scholars of Kashi the greatness of the philosophy of Vishistadwait and that Almighty God Supreme exists in form. Even at this tender age, the divine glory, intelligence and knowledge of Ghanshyam was all evident.

Departure of Parents

Ghanshyam lovingly served and attended to both parents. He wanted to leave for pilgrimage at the time of the Yagnopavit ceremony, but did not for the sake of His parents.

Ghanshyam's mother, Bhaktimata, left her mortal body when He was aged 10 years and 7 months. Prior to the departure of Bhaktimata, Ghanshyam gave her spiritual and philosophical knowledge of Almighty God Supreme. This knowledge is known as Hari Gita. His father, Dharmadev, left his mortal body just seven months after the death of His mother.

When Bhaktimata and Dharmadev left their mortal bodies and departed for Akshardham, Ghanshyam gave them divine darshan of Himself. Both His parents knew that their son was Almighty God Supreme and spiritually remained with Him on earth.

Pilgrimage – Van Vicharan

Ghanshyam always wanted to lead a life of penance, self-control and well being towards mankind. Ghanshyam had observed that religious principles had dissolved and that people were no longer righteous in their behaviour. People manipulated scriptures for their personal benefits, evil forces and demons pervaded and ruled society.

Once Ghanshyam's parents had departed to Akshardham, He

decided to go on pilgrimage to rid evil and establish moral behaviour in society. He wanted to teach people how to lead a moral and righteous life and give them darshan of His divine spirit.

On the 10th day of the bright half of Ashadh month VS 1849, early in the morning Ghanshyam went to the Saryu River in Ayodhya. He was aged 11 years, 3 months and 1 day. Ghanshyam departed from Ayodhya by swimming deep into the river and emerging at another location, He headed for the Himalayas. Ghanshyam started His pilgrimage (Van Vicharan) here and was now known by the name of Nilkanth Varni.

Nilkanth Varni took with Him the following items; kanthi, tulsi mala, deerskin, kamandal (water pot), bowl, gutko (small notebook), undergarment, waist wraparound garment, waist rope, stick and Shaligram purse.

Nilkanth Varni visited the main centres of pilgrimage in North India of Haridwar, Badrinath, Kedarnath, Gangotri and Yamnotri.

Pulhashram

Nilkanth Varni travelled for 3 days in waist high water in caves against the flow of water. Finally He reached Pulhashram. Here Nilkanth Varni undertook severe penance for four months during the monsoon season to impress Surya Narayan, who then came to have darshan of Nilkanth Varni. Through this extreme penance the body of Nilkanth Varni became extremely frail.

Nilkanth Varni undertaking severe penance

The divine forms of Bhaktimata, Dharmadev, Shiva, Parvati, Hanuman, Naradji, Uddhavji and sages came to Pulhashram to have darshan of Nilkanth Varni.

Butolnagar

A year had passed since Nilkanth Varni had left home and He arrived in the town of Butolnagar in Nepal. Mahadatta, the King of Butolnagar, welcomed Nilkanth to his kingdom. The King was attracted to the luminous personality of Nilkanth. The King offered Nilkanth his throne and the King's sister, Mayarani, offered her two daughters in marriage to Nilkanth Varni. Nilkanth Varni declined both and continued on His journey.

Gopalyogi

Nilkanth Varni travelled into the dense forest and jungle. In the jungle He met Gopalyogi, who was adept in the art of Ashtang yoga. Nilkanth Varni stayed with Gopalyogi, respected him and learned yoga from him. Nilkanth revealed His divine form to Gopalyogi during His stay. On the death of Gopalyogi, Nilkanth Varni Himself performed the funeral rights of Gopalyogi.

Seerpur

Nilkanth Varni arrived in Seerpur. The King of Seerpur was Siddh Vallabh. He had great respect for all sadhus, but failed to differentiate between good and bad.

In Seerpur, there were many sadhus who had many vices and lacked belief in God. The sadhus were always keen to impress the King of Seerpur. Historically during the rainy season, sadhus would do penance in the open rain to impress the King. It rained heavily for seven days and only Nilkanth was able to continue penance in such harsh conditions, the other sadhus could not cope.

The King realised that the other sadhus were spiritually and morally weak. He realised that Nilkanth Varni was none other than the divine form of Almighty God Supreme.

Pibek

Nilkanth Varni went to a village in the Assam region. There lived Pibek who was a keen believer and master of witchcraft and evil forms. Pibek saw Nilkanth as his enemy and invoked evil spirits in an attempt to kill Nilkanth.

The evil spirits could not touch the divine form of Nilkanth and in turn attacked Pibek. Nilkanth showed mercy and intervened to save the life of Pibek. Pibek realised that the young Nilkanth was Supreme God.

Nav-Lakha Mountain

Nilkanth Varni arrived at Nav-Lakha Mountain, now known as the Chittagong Hills in Bengal. On the mountain there were 900,000 sages doing penance to their own divine spirit. Here Nilkanth Varni gave darshan of His own divine presence to all the sages at the same time. All the sages realised that Nilkanth Varni was Almighty God Supreme.

Jagannathpuri

Nilkanth Varni then travelled to Jagannathpuri in the state of Orissa. There were many wicked persons dressed as saints living in Jagannathpuri. They led a life of unrighteousness and had many vices. On seeing Nilkanth Varni the wicked persons were impressed at His divine personality. Some of

the wicked persons wanted Nilkanth to join their group, but Nilkanth would have none of it.

With time, the wicked persons became divided amongst themselves. Between them they fought a long and great quarrel where many of the wicked persons were killed and numerous fled. The wicked persons died through their own evil actions.

It was in Jagannathpuri, that the first recitation of the Satsangijeevan took place. Suvratmuni recited the entire Satsangijeevan to Pratapsinh Raja at the bank of the Indradhyum Lake in Jagannathpuri.

Manaspur

Nilkanth Varni then arrived in the town of Manaspur in Orissa. The King of Manaspur, Shatradharma welcomed Nilkanth Varni to the royal palace.

The wicked persons that had escaped from the fighting in Jagannathpuri had come to Manaspur. The wicked persons now saw Nilkanth as their enemy and a trouble causer. In an attempt to kill Nilkanth Varni the wicked persons attacked Nilkanth by throwing stones at Him whilst He meditated. The stones formed a protective dome around Nilkanth and did not harm Him at all.

The King saw the evil actions of the wicked persons and punished them. The King also realised that Nilkanth Varni was Almighty God Supreme Himself.

Shreerangam, South India

Nilkanth Varni arrived in Shreerangam and stayed there for two months. Shreerangam is the main centre of Shree Ramanuj Acharya. Ramanuj Acharya was the guru of Ramanand Swami and had initiated Him.

Rameshwaram

Nilkanth Varni arrived in Rameshwaram, where one of the twelve jyoti lingas are located. Lord Ram had built a bridge from Rameshwaram to Lanka to conquer the demon Ravana and rescue His wife Sita.

Dense Forest, South India

On leaving Rameshwaram, Nilkanth Varni walked through the dense forest of South India without food and water for five days. On the sixth day of travelling, He found a well and sat down to do Pooja of Shaligram. As He bathed Shaligram, Shaligram drank a lot of water due to thirst.

Lord Shiva and Parvati came for darshan of Nilkanth Varni in the forest. Knowing that Nilkanth Varni had not eaten for several days, they offered sathavo (food comprising of seven different grain types) to Nilkanth Varni.

Loj

Having travelled across all the corners of India for 7 years, 1 month and 11 days, Nilkanth Varni finally arrived in Gujarat, in the town of Loj on the 6th day of the dark half of the month of Shravan 1856, aged 18. He arrived at Loj in the morning and sat beside the step well in the town. There He ended His epic Van Vicharan.

In Loj, there was an ashram of Ramanand Swami. Muktanand Swami was the head saint at the ashram. Sukhanand Swami, a disciple of Ramanand Swami saw Nilkanth Varni doing meditation at the step well. Sukhanand Swami was amazed on seeing the luminous personality of Nilkanth. Sukhanand Swami approached Nilkanth and asked Him, "Dear Varni, where do you come from and where are you going?"

Nilkanth Varni replied, "I have come from Brahmpur (heaven) and I am going to Brahmpur." Sukhanand Swami was astounded by the greatness of Nilkanth, he persuaded Nilkanth to go to their ashram. Here, Nilkanth met Muktanand Swami who asked Him to stay.

Nilkanth Varni said that He could only stay in that ashram if Muktanand Swami could satisfactorily answer His questions. He asked Muktanand Swami, "What is Jeeva, Ishwar, Maya, Brahm and Parbrahm?" Muktanand Swami was astounded at the quality of questions posed by young Nilkanth Varni.

Muktanand Swami answered, "Jeeva is the eternal soul that cannot be destroyed, Ishwar is the form of Demi-God, Maya is the force of God distracting one's devotion, Brahm is the jeeva that has achieved salvation and Parbrahm is the Almighty God Supreme Himself."

Throughout His journey across India, no one had previously been able to provide satisfactory answers to these questions. Nilkanth Varni was pleased with Muktanand Swami's answer and therefore decided to stay in Loj.

Meeting of Ramanand Swami and Initiation

Saryudas

Nilkanth Varni stayed in Loj, working and serving in the ashram of Ramanand Swami. Here in Loj Muktanand Swami gave Nilkanth Varni another name, Saryudas. The meaning being that Nilkanth Varni had come from across the River Saryu in Ayodhya. From this point onwards Nilkanth Varni was now referred to as Saryudas.

Saryudas, even being Almighty God Supreme, displayed qualities that an ideal disciple should have. Here in the ashram at Loj, Saryudas used to do many menial duties including cleaning the ashram, collecting cow dung for fuel and feeding the poor.

Saryudas was very learned in yoga. In Loj He taught yoga to all the disciples of the ashram.

Separate Assemblies

In the ashram at Loj, males and females sat together during prayers and religious assemblies. On seeing this, Saryudas strongly opposed the mixed assemblies. He explained that He had observed many great saints and satsangis that had fallen in religion through contact with the opposite sex. He therefore stopped the gathering of mixed assemblies from this point onwards.

Hole in the Wall 'Gokhlo'

In the Ashram at Loj there was a hole in the wall between the ashram and the neighbouring building, a barber's house.

Through this hole, saints would take smouldering coal for cooking purposes and other items also. Frequently the saints would have contact with women through the gokhlo.

Saryudas objected to the saints having contact with women. Saryudas stated that in order to observe strict celibacy and maintain their strong attachment to God, saints must not have contact with females. Saryudas got the hole between the ashram and the barber's home filled in.

Letter to Ramanand Swami

Saryudas was eager to meet Ramanand Swami, Head of the ashram at Loj and the guru of Muktanand Swami. He was temporarily residing at the home of Gangaram Mull in Bhuj.

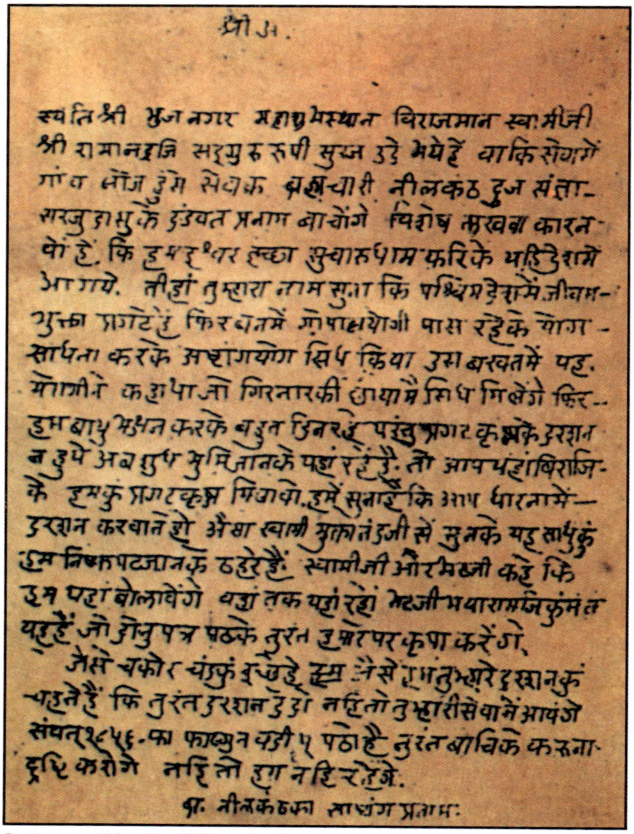
श्री ॥

स्वस्ति श्री भुजनगर महाशुभस्थान विराजमान स्वामीजी
श्री रामानंदजी सद्गुरु रूपी सूरज उदे भये हैं याकि सेवामें
गांव लोज दुंगे सेवक ब्रह्मचारी नीलकंठ दुज संता-
सरजुदासकु दंडवत प्रनाम बांचोगे विशेष लखवा कारन
यों है कि हम ईश्वर इच्छा से धामरूप करिके यहिं देशमें
आ गये. तहां तुम्हारा नाम सुना कि पश्चिम देशमें जीवन-
मुक्त प्रगटे हैं फिर बनमें गोपालयोगी पास रहके योग-
साधना करके अष्टांगयोग सिध किया उस वखतमें यह
योगीने कहा था जो गिरनारकी छायामें सिध मिलेंगे फिर
हम बहु भ्रमन करके बहुत दिन रहे परंतु प्रगट कृष्णके दरशन
न हुए अब दुध मुक्तानंदके यहां रहे हैं. तो आप यहां बिराजि-
के हमकुं प्रगट कृष्ण मिलावो. हमें सुनाई कि आप धारनामें
दरशन करवाते हो ऐसा स्वामी मुक्तानंदजी से सुनके यह साधुकुं
हम निष्कपटजानके ठहरे हैं. स्वामीजी और भक्तजी कहे कि
हम यहां बोलावेंगे वहां तक यहां रहो भक्तजी भयारामजिकुं मंत
यह है जो ऐसु पत्र पढके तुरंत हमारे पर कृपा करेंगे.
जैसे चकोर चंद्रकुं देखे हम ऐसे ही तुम्हारे दरशनकुं
चहते हैं कि तुरंत दरशन दुआ नहि तो तुम्हारी सेवामें आयंगे
संवत १८५६-का फाल्गुन वदी ५ पठा है तुरंत बांचिके करुना-
दृष्टि करोगे नहि तो हम नहि रहेंगे.

ब्र. नीलकंठका साष्टांग प्रनाम:

Letter written by Nilkanth Varni

Saryudas asked Muktanand Swami for permission to go to Bhuj to meet Ramanand Swami. Muktanand Swami persuaded Saryudas to reside in Loj and instead Muktanand Swami and Saryudas each wrote a letter to Ramanand Swami. Mayaram Bhatt personally took the letters to Ramanand Swami in Bhuj.

Ramanand Swami received the letters of Muktanand Swami and Saryudas. He opened the letter from Saryudas, as he did this the room filled with a brilliant shining light.

On reading the letter, Ramanand Swami explained to the satsangis around him that, "I am only a servant, Almighty God Himself has arrived in all His divine glory. I have been waiting for Him and now He has arrived."

Ramanand Swami wrote back to Saryudas asking Him to stay in Loj, serving at the ashram and that he would meet Him soon.

Meeting of Saryudas and Ramanand Swami in Piplana

After a period of 9 months in Loj, Saryudas received a message from Ramanand Swami through a satsangi, Kunverjibhai. Ramanand Swami asked Saryudas, Muktanand Swami and other saints and satsangis to meet him at Piplana near Junagadh.

Saryudas, Muktanand Swami and others arrived in Piplana on the 12th day of the dark half of the month Jeth VS 1856 at the residence of Narsinh Mehta, where Ramanand Swami was staying after arriving from Bhuj.

On seeing Saryudas, Ramanand Swami got up from his feet and heartily and lovingly embraced Him, realising that He was Almighty God Supreme. Ramanand Swami asked Saryudas about His parents, His childhood and His pilgrimage that led Him to Loj.

Maha Bhagwati Diksha Ceremony in Jetpur

Five months after meeting Ramanand Swami, Saryudas was initiated in a grand ceremony, Maha Bhagwati Diksha in Jetpur.

On Prabodhini Ekadashi, the 11th day on the bright half of the month of Kartik VS 1857 Ramanand Swami initiated Saryudas. Saryudas was given the names of Sahajanand Swami and Narayan Muni by Ramanand Swami. From this point onwards Saryudas was referred to by the name of Sahajanand Swami.

Sahajanand Swami throned as Leader

Exactly a year after initiating Sahajanand Swami, Ramanand Swami throned Sahajanand Swami as the leader of the Sampraday in Jetpur. He did this because Sahajanand Swami was none other than Almighty God Himself.

Ramanand Swami wanted to hand the throne of the Sampraday to Sahajanand Swami. Ramanand Swami held a meeting with the prominent saints and satsangis, to nominate a suitable successor. Ramanand Swami himself nominated Sahajanand Swami to become leader, instantly Muktanand Swami joyously agreed and other members also accepted this.

Sahajanand Swami initially declined to accept the throne. Ramanand Swami urged him to take the throne as he himself was old and only He (Sahajanand Swami) was capable. Sahajanand Swami took responsibility of the satsang at the young age of 20 years and 7 months.

Boons, to protect the followers of the Sampraday

Ramanand Swami was extremely pleased that Sahajanand Swami accepted the throne and granted Sahajanand Swami all His wishes.

Sahajanand Swami asked Ramanand Swami for two requests:

> *"If a follower of the sampraday suffers the pain of a scorpion sting, that pain must befall on Me millions upon millions of times, but the satsangi of this sampraday should enjoy peace."*
>
> *"If a follower of the sampraday has to suffer hardship of getting food and clothes, and has to beg according to his fate, I beg those hardships befall on Me and the satsangi should get food and clothes easily."*

Ramanand Swami was enlightened by the requests of Sahajanand Swami and lovingly embraced Him. The significance of these boons is infinite and is unique to the Swaminarayan Sampraday. It shows the love that Sahajanand Swami has for His devotees.

Departure of Ramanand Swami

One month and one day after Sahajanand Swami accepted the throne, Ramanand Swami gathered an assembly in Faneni near Jetpur. Ramanand Swami said to the saints and satsangis present, "I am Uddhavji, Sahajanand Swami is Almighty God Supreme and you must all serve and obey Him for ultimate salvation. I have achieved all that I came for."

Ramanand Swami closed his eyes and started meditation. Here he left his mortal body on the 13th day of the bright half of the month of Magsar VS 1858. Sahajanand Swami Himself performed the funeral ceremony.

Lord Swaminarayan, Almighty God Supreme

Fourteen days after the passing of Ramanand Swami, Sahajanand Swami held His first sabha in Faneni, mourning the death of Ramanand Swami.

Sahajanand Swami said to the satsangis present, "We have worshipped God by many different names such as Krishna, Narayan etc, but to gain ultimate salvation there should only be one name and form of Almighty God Supreme, that name is Swaminarayan."

Sahajanand Swami asked the whole sabha to chant "Swaminarayan", a single mantra comprising of six syllables, Swa-mi-na-ra-ya-n. From here onwards Sahajanand Swami was known as Swaminarayan, Lord Swaminarayan.

Establishment of Swaminarayan Sampraday

Lord Swaminarayan took responsibility of the sampraday at a young age. Over the next three decades Lord Swaminarayan worked endlessly to rid society of evil and wrong doing. Ultimately He wanted satsangis to lead a peaceful and moral life in order to attain salvation and reach Akshardham.

Over the coming years Lord Swaminarayan established the necessary framework for a strong and ever lasting sampraday. He personally did this by constructing temples, installing idols of God and composing scriptures.

He initiated Acharyas to lead the sampraday and saints to maintain and promote the well being of the sampraday. He demonstrated to all human beings how one should lead a moral and peaceful life.

Aarti of Lord by Muktanand Swami

Muktanand Swami was the leading saint of Ramanand Swami's satsang. He was older than Lord Swaminarayan and Lord Swaminarayan treated him as a guru and with great respect.

Muktanand Swami had found out that many satsangis coming for darshan of Lord Swaminarayan would enter into a spiritual trance, by merely looking at Lord. Muktanand Swami could not believe these actions of Lord Swaminarayan. Muktanand Swami thought Lord Swaminarayan did not have this power or authority. Muktanand Swami spoke to Lord Swaminarayan and questioned Him, but Lord said nothing to him.

In the following morning Ramanand Swami gave Muktanand Swami divine darshan and said to him, "I told you before that I am a humble servant of Almighty God Supreme and the divine power is within Sahajanand Swami Himself and He is capable of anything and everything." It was then that Muktanand Swami realised that Lord Swaminarayan was Almighty God Supreme and with an instant all his doubts were eradicated.

His love and bond towards Lord Swaminarayan was infinite. Muktanand Swami being an accomplished poet could not contain his love for Lord and compiled the words to the aarti in the town of Kalwani. He prostrated and sang the aarti to Lord, "Jay Sadguru Swami..."

Lord assumes double form in Aakha and Piplana

Aakha and Piplana are two villages separated by a river in Gujarat. On one occasion Lord Swaminarayan met satsangis of each village in Kalwani. The satsangis each requested Lord to come to their village and perform large yagnas.

Lord Swaminarayan was pulled from two directions at the same time as both villages wanted to have His presence and blessings for a yagna. To please satsangis from both villages Lord Swaminarayan performed a spectacular miracle in these villages.

Lord Swaminarayan and all his accompanying saints and satsangis took double form for a period of six months. So Lord Swaminarayan, saints and satsangis with Him became two and went to the villages of Aakha and Piplana simultaneously to conduct grand yagnas at each village.

This miracle only came to light when a satsangi from Aakha came to Piplana. He was astonished to see Lord Swaminarayan and His followers all in Piplana conducting a yagna, since he had just seen them all in Aakha a short time earlier.

These were the miracles Lord Swaminarayan performed to please His followers.

Final sacrificial yagna

On the 9th day of the bright half of the month of Chaitra VS 1860, the birthday of Lord Swaminarayan, He arrived in Bhuj and stayed at the home of Sundarji Suthar. Lord was 23 years of age.

In Bhuj, Jagjeevan, advisor to the King of Bhuj was holding a massive sacrificial yagna. Jagjeevan invited Lord Swaminarayan to the yagna. On arriving at the yagna, Lord Swaminarayan observed that Jagjeevan planned to sacrifice hundreds of animals as offering to the Gods.

Lord Swaminarayan said to all present that killing living creatures is not permitted under Vedic law, whether it be for food or sacrificial purposes. Jagjeevan insulted Lord Swaminarayan by still pursuing with the sacrificial yagna.

At this point the King of Bhuj intervened. He questioned Jagjeevan about holding such a large yagna. Jagjeevan could not justify his reasons or the costs incurred. As he was abusing his role in his duty to the King, the King of Bhuj stopped the yagna and forced his army on Jagjeevan, this resulted in the death of Jagjeevan.

In the aftermath of the yagna the message of Lord Swaminarayan of ahimsa and non-violence in yagna ceremonies became widespread and fully accepted. Thereafter no animals were killed for sacrifice at yagnas.

Gadhada

Lord Swaminarayan first came to Gadhada on the 11th day of the bright half of the month of Magsar in VS 1861.

The King of Gadhada was Ebhelkhachar (father of Dadakhachar), who went to take darshan of Lord in Kariyani and had realised that He was none other than God. Ebhelkhachar invited Lord to visit Gadhada, Lord stated that He would follow afterwards. Ebhelkhachar personally wanted to accompany Lord to Gadhada from Kariyani and therefore stayed with Him until the day He was ready to come. On Lord's arrival to Gadhada, Ebhelkhachar graciously received him and asked Lord Swaminarayan to stay there with his family.

Ebhelkhachar felt extremely humble and fortunate to be blessed with the presence of Lord Swaminarayan. Within a short time he handed over all his wealth and the royal palace in Gadhada to Lord before passing away. The main palace in Gadhada is known as 'Dadakhachar's Darbar.' A courtyard is the focal point of the darbar and at the centre of the courtyard there has always been a neem (limbdo) tree.

Lord Swaminarayan made Gadhada His home, centre of the divine sampraday and stayed here for most of His life. Lord Swaminarayan conducted hundreds of assemblies in the courtyard, royal rooms and verandas.

A significant proportion of the Vachnamrit discourses took place in Dadakhachar's Darbar. Both the Satsangijeevan and Bhaktachintamani scriptures were written in Gadhada in the presence of Lord Swaminarayan.

Lord Swaminarayan reunited with His brothers

Lord Swaminarayan had left His family at a young age. On settling in Gujarat He had lost contact with His brothers and their families.

To regain contact, He sent Mayatitanand Swami to search for His brothers, Rampratapji and Iccharamji, in the region of Ayodhya. After searching high and low Mayatitanand Swami located and found the brothers of Lord Swaminarayan.

Rampratapji and Iccharamji came to Gujarat with their families and were reunited with their Brother, Lord Swaminarayan in Vadtal after 26 years of separation. Rampratapji, Iccharamji and their families thereafter stayed with Lord Swaminarayan.

Debate of Vadodara

Vadodara was a city famous for being a centre and focal point of great scholars. There were many scholars residing in Vadodara who did not accept that Lord Swaminarayan was Almighty God Supreme. The satsangis of Vadodara could not tolerate this and they visited Lord Swaminarayan and explained the situation to Him in Vadtal.

On hearing the difficulty of the satsangis of Vadodara, Lord Swaminarayan decided to send Muktanand Swami to Vadodara to prove to the scholars that Lord Swaminarayan was God.

Muktanand Swami attended a large assembly in Vadodara arranged by the King of Vadodara, named Siyaji Rao. Here many scholars doubting Lord Swaminarayan had gathered.

The debate between the scholars and Muktanand Swami commenced. The scholars posed numerous questions to Muktanand Swami, interrogating the existence of Lord Swaminarayan as God. Muktanand Swami answered each question to prove that Lord Swaminarayan was none other than Almighty God Supreme. Each answer was fully supported by direct reference to Vedic scriptures including Shreemad Bhagwad Gita, Shreemad Bhagwat and the Vedas.

All the scholars accepted defeat and Muktanand Swami was hailed victorious. It was here that the chairman of the meeting, Bhaupurani pronounced, "Swaminarayano Vijaytetram". This saying is frequently used in our sampraday and means 'Victory to Lord Swaminarayan'.

Lord's final farewell

Residing in Gadhada Lord Swaminarayan had established a strong sampraday. He had achieved all He had come to earth for and therefore decided it was now right for Him to return to Akshardham.

Lord Swaminarayan knew that the saints and satsangis would suffer indescribable pain on His departure, so many would plead Him to stay and some would prevent Him from leaving .

Lord Swaminarayan told Brahmanand Swami to go to Junagadh and oversee the completion of the temple construction. Brahmanand Swami instinctively realised that Lord Swaminarayan would leave His mortal body and go to Akshardham, whilst he was in Junagadh. Brahmanand Swami did not want to go but could not disobey an order from Lord and he left for Junagadh. Before leaving, Brahmanand Swami told Gopalanand Swami not to cremate Lord's body if He departed this world. Brahmanand Swami said this because he had such great powers that he would bring Lord back to this earth if Lord's body had not been cremated.

Lord Swaminarayan told Gopalanand Swami of His intention to leave His mortal body. Gopalanand Swami was given the overall responsibility of the sampraday and specifically told him not to inform Brahmanand Swami until His mortal body had been cremated. Here Lord Swaminarayan held the hands of both Acharyas and asked Gopalanand Swami to take care of both of them.

Lord Swaminarayan called a meeting of all saints and satsangis present and said, "I have fully completed all My intentions for coming to earth. I will now return to Akshardham. I promise you I will be ever present here on earth, through My idols, scriptures, acharyas and saints. You must all remain strong and not come after Me by committing suicide."

On hearing this, saints and satsangis exploded into cries of pain and loss. The sense of loss was indescribable. Lord

Swaminarayan sat down with prominent saints and servants, closed His eyes and peacefully left His mortal body and returned to Akshardham, on the 10th day of the bright half of the month of Jeth VS 1886 (1st June 1830 AD), aged 49 years 2 months and 1 day,

Lord's body was prepared for cremation and was taken to the grounds of Laxmiwadi in Gadhada. Here the Acharyas, Ayodhyaprasadji and Raghuvirji cremated Lord Swaminarayan. Today, a pious temple stands in Laxmiwadi at the site of Lord's cremation.

Saints and satsangis could not bear the pain of seeing Lord being cremated. Dadakhachar could not bear being separated from Lord, he rushed to jump on the funeral pyre, but was held back by Gopalanand Swami who told Dadakhachar to go to the mango tree in Laxmiwadi where Lord frequently held assemblies.

On reaching the mango tree, the spiritual form of Lord Swaminarayan embraced Dadakhachar and placed a rose garland over him and said, "Dada, do you think I have gone? No, I am ever present and will always be here."

Brahmanand Swami found out that Lord had departed to Akshardham and returned to Gadhada. Brahmanand Swami asked Gopalanand Swami, "Why did you cremate Lord before I returned to Gadhada?" Gopalanand Swami replied, "It was Lord's wish that I called you after He had been cremated, since Lord knew that otherwise you would have brought Him back to earth."

In great distress Brahmanand Swami went to pray to Gopinathji Maharaj, at Gadhada temple. As Brahmanand Swami reached the temple, Lord Swaminarayan gave Brahmanand Swami divine darshan and said, "I have not left, I am still here."

Lord Swaminarayan

Lord Swaminarayan has been and always will be described as being beautiful in His appearance. He is described in every Vachnamrit as to what He was wearing e.g. a white turban, a garland of white flowers etc. This depiction, which has been written down by honourable saints enables satsangis to visualise the divine image of Lord Swaminarayan.

All Swaminarayan temples have images of Lord Swaminarayan. This helps the satsangis to be closer to God by meditation and imagining what Lord Swaminarayan would be wearing in Akshardham. The main painters and sculptors during Lord Swaminarayan's time were Adharanand Swami and Narayanji Suthar. Their portraits of Lord can still be seen today.

Lord's daily routine

Each day Lord Swaminarayan woke up around 4:30am in the morning. He always had Brahmcharis to help with His daily routine. He brushed His teeth with a daatan, which He then split into two pieces and used it as a tongue cleaner.

This daatan was usually prepared the night before and placed in a jar with cardamom seeds (elachi). Whatever He wore at night was what He bathed in the following morning.

After bathing He would wring out His dhoti and wipe the lower parts of His body. He would then put on a new dhoti and use the bathing dhoti to wipe the rest of His body.

He would then put on clean fresh clothes. After bathing He meditated and then had a light snack, which was prepared by the Brahmcharis. The two main servants that were always with Lord Swaminarayan were Bhaguji and Mulji Brahmchari.

Lord's appearance

Lord Swaminarayan wore beautiful clothes, white coloured clothes were His favourite, but He occasionally wore colourful clothes too. He adorned gold necklaces and garlands of flowers. His turban had decorative toras (flower arrangements on the turban), which were woven on to the

turban. The turban would have three or four chhoglas (tassels). Lord Swaminarayan would almost always have a flower behind His ear. He wore gajras and baju-bands made of flowers on the wrists and arms respectively.

Lord Swaminarayan was 5 feet 4 ¼ inches tall. He had bow shaped eyebrows, eyes with the shape of lotus petals and His nose had a slight dip. All these features made Lord Swaminarayan have the most perfect face.

Lord's habits and behaviour

Lord Swaminarayan possessed divine qualities and mannerisms. His personality was truly special. Lord Swaminarayan was very jovial with all satsangis and saints. He would often joke with others and engage in playful activities.

Lord Swaminarayan had different and unusual ways of sitting. During sabha Lord Swaminarayan had a habit of sitting with His leg over His thigh. When He ate He always sat facing north or east, with His right leg raised, upon which He rested His right arm and with His left leg flat on the floor.

Whilst He sat He would stroke the creases (Urdhvarekhas) in His feet using His first and second finger. When He sneezed or coughed He would always place a handkerchief over His mouth and nose, and would chant 'Hare...Hare...Hare...' after doing so. When He got up after sitting down He would chant, Jay Sachidanand or Jay Swaminarayan.

Since Lord Swaminarayan performed a lot of gatherings (sabhas), this was the best opportunity for people to see His unique manners and habits. During sabhas, He would use a tulsi mala one bead at a time or maybe two beads at a time or sometimes He would just play with the mala. He would often put cold lemons or mogra flowers to His eyes and nose to cool and soothe them.

During His sabhas or on travelling, if He saw poor and sick people, He would show extreme compassion towards them and He would give away His precious belongings without hesitation. When satsangis arrived for darshan, the Lord would always ask their names, where they were from and asked after their well being.

In sabhas when saints were singing kirtans, He would join in and sway with the rhythm of the singing and the sound of musical instruments. When Lord became extremely pleased with satsangis or saints, He would get up in the middle of the sabha and lovingly embrace those sparkling individuals.

Lord Swaminarayan had a very brisk and elegant style of walking. People walking with Him would struggle to keep up with Him. Lord Swaminarayan always kept a handkerchief in His hand and as He walked He would lightly tap His right thigh with His right fist.

Lord's Cheens

Distinct features made Lord Swaminarayan unique and divine. He had many beauty spots all over His body. These features and cheens are those that only Almighty God Supreme would possess.

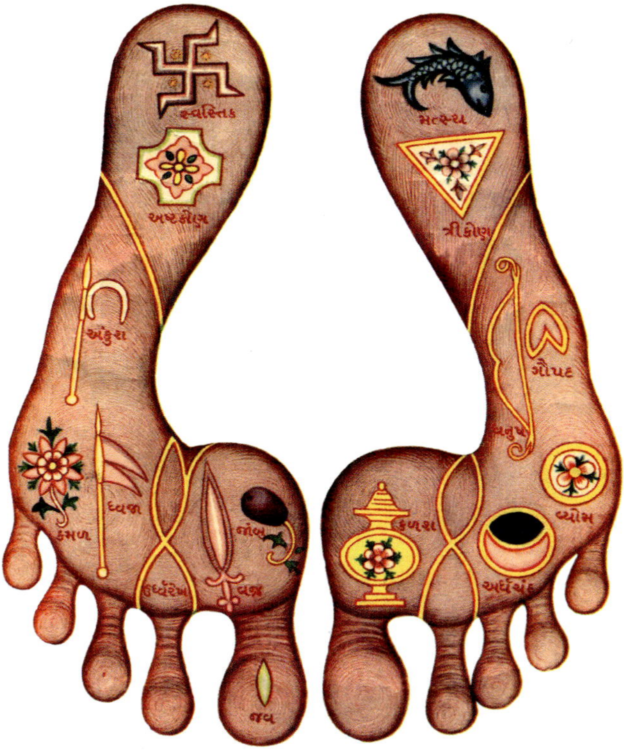

Lotus feet of Lord Swaminarayan

The Lord has sixteen symbolic icons on His Lotus Feet, with nine cheens on His right foot and seven on His left foot. These cheens are unique to Almighty God and no other human being on the earth possesses such features. One can recognise Almighty God Supreme by observing His divine Lotus Feet.

One gains guidance and help to the path of righteousness and salvation through meditating and focusing upon the Lotus Feet of Lord. Nishkulanand Swami examined the qualities of each cheen. One achieves the following results of the mind and soul through meditation upon each cheen.

Right Foot Cheens

	*Swastik*	Good luck.
	*Ashtakon (Octagon)*	Easily able to overcome hardship arising from the elements of the universe.
	*Ankush (Goad)*	Control over mind and senses, in the same way an elephant owner controls his elephant by using the ankush.
	*Kamal (Lotus)*	Constant focus on Lord Swaminarayan is achieved, forces of maya are kept at bay, just as the lotus flower remains on water.
	*Ketu (Flag)*	Guided through life with the principles of Lord Shree Swaminarayan, in the same way that wind guides the sway and direction of a flag.
	*Urdhva-Rekha (Ascendant Line)*	Attainment of salvation.
	*Vajra (Sword)*	Inner negative forces and evils are overcome.
	*Jambu (Blackberry)*	Liberated from the desire of taste.
	*Java (Barley grain)*	Attainment of inner tranquility and eradication of sins.

Left Foot Cheens

Matsya (Fish)

Permanent and inseparable bond developed with Lord Swaminarayan. In the same way that a fish cannot live without water.

Trikon (Triangle)

The three forms of suffering, being mental suffering, suffering imposed by other beings and natural hardships are eliminated.

Gaupad (Cow foot print)

Easily able to break away from the cycle of birth and death, in the same way that one is able to easily stride over the foot print of a cow.

Dhanush (Bow)

Inner enemies are overcome.

Vyom (Space)

The heart remains pure and does not get polluted by worldly objects and pleasures, in the same way that space remains pure.

Ardha Chandra (Half moon)

State of calmness attained in the heart at all times, in the same way that the moon always appears calm and at peace.

Kalash (Holy Pot)

Goal of salvation and aims in life are attained.

Acharyas, heads of the sampraday

> *"Rampratapji and Iccharamji, both of Shree Dharmadev, are My brothers. Rampratapji's son, Ayodhyaprasad and Iccharamji's son Raghuvir, both of whom I have adopted as My sons and established them as the Acharyas of My disciples."*
>
> *(Shikshapatri Sloka 3)*

The Acharyas of the Swaminarayan Sampraday act as a focal point and figureheads for all saints and devotees. The system of an Acharya leading a religion is not unique to the Swaminarayan sampraday, but is common in various branches of Hinduism.

The True Swaminarayan sampraday is that, which is only ultimately headed by the Acharyas, falling under the diocese of NarNarayan Dev or LaxmiNarayan Dev.

> *"My disciples shall worship only those idols of Shree Krishna which are given to them by the Acharyas, or installed by him. They shall bow down respectfully to other idols but shall not worship them."*
>
> *(Shikshapatri Sloka 62)*

Acharyas must be householders and not saints

Lord Swaminarayan realised that it was essential to have Acharyas to take position as heads of the sampraday. It was a big decision to make for Lord Swaminarayan, whether He should have householders or saints as the Acharyas.

A person becomes a saint on renouncing the material world, its objects and its affairs. Saints aim to give religious discourses, knowledge and guidance of followers of that religion and not become involved in material matters and issues.

During His pilgrimage Lord Swaminarayan travelled far and wide in India. During this time He determined that for a saint to remain unaffected by worldly matters they should avoid contact with wealth and women, thus ensuring a life of devotion is led.

Lord Swaminarayan, with other great saints decided only a householder was suitable for the position of Acharya. Since, by the nature of the role of Acharya, he would be in contact with wealth, women and material issues on many occasions and therefore saints would not be suitable for this role.

Lord Swaminarayan elected Acharyas from the Dharmadev family

Devotees and saints of Lord Swaminarayan saw Him in His divine glory and form during His presence on earth. Devotees and saints looked upon the family of Dharmadev with divine love and respect since Lord Swaminarayan Himself had manifested into that family.

It was for this reason that Lord Swaminarayan chose two

householders from the family of His father Dharmadev, who were blood relations to Himself. It seemed only natural to elect Acharyas from the family of Dharmadev that had the divine link to Lord Swaminarayan. The head saints, Muktanand Swami, Gopalanand Swami and Nityanand Swami unanimously supported this decision.

Creation of two Acharyas and diocese

The Swaminarayan sampraday had rapidly grown during the divine presence of Lord Swaminarayan, and would continue to do so after His departure. The work of Acharya would have been too great for any one person. Lord Swaminarayan along with prominent saints determined that India should be divided to enable easier management of the sampraday.

Shree Ayodhyaprasadji

Shree Raghuvirji

India was therefore divided into two regions. A demarcation line was drawn between Kolkata and Dwarika. North of this boundary known as the Uttar desh (North diocese – NarNarayan Dev), and south of the boundary became Dakshin desh (South Diocese - LaxmiNarayan Dev). Lord Swaminarayan outlined the full jurisdiction of each Acharya in the document called Desh Vibhag Lekh.

Acharyas of Ahmedabad and Vadtal diocese

Lord Swaminarayan at Ahmedabad and Vadtal had constructed large temples. Lord installed murtis of Shree

NarNarayan Dev and Shree LaxmiNarayan Dev at the temples respectively. These two cities became the centre for each diocese.

Ahmedabad became the centre of the Uttar desh and was named NarNarayan Dev Gadi. Vadtal became the centre of the Dakshin desh and was named LaxmiNarayan Dev Gadi. A complete list of the Acharyas of both Gadi's is included in the reference section.

Role of Acharyas

When Lord Swaminarayan left His mortal body and returned to Akshardham, He personally left the responsibility of the sampraday in the hands of the two Acharyas, along with guidance from head saints and satsangis.

Lord Swaminarayan authorised the two Acharyas to install murtis of God in His temples and perform the ceremonies and rituals at these temples. Lord Swaminarayan clearly stated that He would only reside in the murtis at temples, where the Acharyas had performed the initiation ceremonies.

Only Acharyas have been given the role to initiate saints and devotees. Saints do not have the authority to initiate devotees. Acharyas are only permitted to initiate male devotees, and are prohibited from initiating female members of the sampraday. The Acharyas are not allowed to meet and talk to female members of the sampraday. The Acharya's wife performs the role of initiating female devotees.

Desh Vibhag Lekh

The Desh Vibhag Lekh represents the constitution of the Swaminarayan sampraday. Lord personally dictated the Lekh and had it written on the full moon day of the month of Magsar in the VS 1883 (1827 AD). Lord then presented the lekh to saints, devotees and the Acharyas.

The Lekh pays particular attention to the roles and responsibility of the Acharyas. In particular, it mentions the management of the sampraday, demarcation of the two dioceses and suitability of Acharyas.

Lord Swaminarayan stated that the Acharya must be a direct descendant of the Dharmadev family. The Acharyaship is not purely hereditary, but based on inheritance and merit. The Acharya should be learned, pious, virtuous, moral, ardent and be a staunch devotee of Lord Swaminarayan.

Temples

In all religions, there is always a focal point to ensure that the faith continues and grows in the future. In Hinduism, temples perform a vital role in acting as a focal point in the sampraday. Lord Swaminarayan recognised that temples would be vital to ensure that the sampraday grew far and wide.

To prevent His devotees from straying away from religion and to keep everyone devoted to Him, Lord Swaminarayan thought of two things. Firstly, to build temples and install idols of Lord Shree Krishna and Himself as Lord Shree HariKrishna Maharaj. Secondly, to write scriptures to reveal the greatness of the Swaminarayan Sampraday.

A man however great or intelligent cannot meditate calmly in the home. The reason is simple, there are many material objects and thoughts in the home that will distract one's devotion. There is a traditional saying that performing one mala at the temple will give the same fruits as doing one hundred malas at home. This illustrates how important temples are in our sampraday.

Lord Himself installed the murtis at the temples that He constructed. After His departure to Akshardham, as Lord had stated that Acharyas should install murtis of God with Vedic mantras and ceremonies.

People achieve great inspiration and pleasure whilst worshipping God with great saints and other devotees in the temple. For these reasons temples are a necessity in the life of a satsangi. Lord Swaminarayan had six temples constructed in His divine presence. These temples were constructed at Ahmedabad, Bhuj, Vadtal, Dholera, Junagadh and Gadhada.

Ahmedabad

Shree NarNarayan Dev

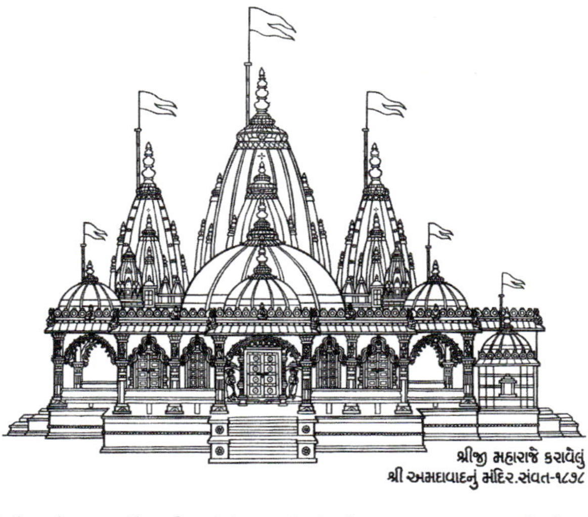

શ્રીજી મહારાજે કરાવેલું
શ્રી અમદાવાદનું મંદિર.સંવત-૧૮૭૮

Ahmedabad was the first temple to be constructed. An English collector gave the land during the British Raj. The deed document was transcribed on to a copper plate, stating that the land would remain under ownership of the Swaminarayan Sampraday for all time.

Anandanand Swami designed the structure of the temple. Lord Swaminarayan Himself installed the images of Lord NarNarayan Dev in VS 1878 on the 3rd day of the bright half of the month of Falgun (Monday 24th February 1822 AD).

Bhuj – Kutch

Shree NarNarayan Dev

શ્રીજી મહારાજે કરાવેલું ભુજનું મંદિર.સંવત-૧૮૭૯

The devotees living in Bhuj including Gangaram Mull, Sundarji Suthar and Hirji Suthar requested Lord to construct a temple at Bhuj.

Lord instructed Vaishnavanand Swami to construct the temple and again Lord himself installed the murti of Lord NarNarayan Dev in Bhuj on VS 1879 on the 5th day of the bright half of the month of Vaishakh (Friday 15th May 1823 AD).

Vadtal

Shree LaxmiNarayan Dev

Devotees of Vadtal including Joban Pagi, Kuberbhai Patel and Ranchodbhai Patel requested Lord to build a huge temple at Vadtal. Brahmanand Swami and Aksharanand Swami designed the Vadtal temple. Lord Swaminarayan Himself helped in the construction of the Vadtal temple by carrying stones to the site.

At Vadtal, Lord installed Shree LaxmiNarayan Dev, Shree Ranchodrai Dev and Shree HariKrishna Maharaj (image of Himself) with Shree RadhaKrishna Dev. Lord installed these images in Vadtal in VS 1881 on the 12th day of the bright half of the month of Kartik (Thursday 3rd November 1823 AD).

Dholera

Shree MadanMohan Dev

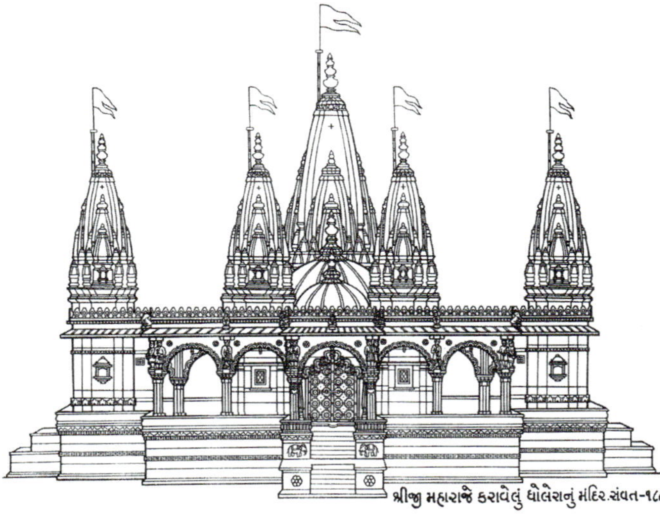

શ્રીજી મહારાજે કરાવેલું ધોલેરાનું મંદિર.સંવત-૧૮૮૨

Punjaji Darbar of Dholera urged Lord to construct a temple in Dholera. Nishkulanand Swami and Adbhutanand Swami constructed the temple. Lord Swaminarayan installed Shree MadanMohan Dev and Radhikaji in VS 1882 on the 13th day of the dark half of the month of Vaishakh (Saturday 19th May 1826 AD).

Junagadh

Shree RadhaRaman Dev

શ્રીજી મહારાજે કરાવેલું
શ્રી જૂનાગઢનું મંદિર.સંવત-૧૮૮૪

Lord constructed a huge temple at Junagadh on land presented by Jinabhai (Hematsinh) Darbar of Panchala. Brahmanand Swami constructed the temple and Lord installed Shree RadhaRaman Dev in VS 1884 on the 2nd day of the bright half of the month of Vaishakh (Friday 1st May 1828 AD).

Gadhada

Shree Gopinathji Maharaj

Lord Swaminarayan stayed in Gadhada for 25 years. He made Gadhada the centre of the sampraday whilst He was on earth. It was the deep love and affection of Dadakhachar and his four sisters Jaya (Jivuba), Lalita (Laduba), Panchali and Nanu (Ramabai) that attracted Lord to spend most of His life in Gadhada. He stayed at the royal residence of Dadakhachar treating it as His personal home.

By the request of Dadakhachar and his sisters, Lord constructed a grand temple under His personal supervision and with the assistance of Viraktanand Swami. At Gadhada temple Lord installed Shree Gopinathji and Radhikaji. The murtis were installed in VS 1885 on the 12th day of the bright half of the month of Ashwin (Saturday 9th October 1828 AD).

The image and murti of Gopinathji Maharaj installed at Gadhada is in the same proportions as the Lord Himself. Narayanji Suthar was the sculptor of the murti of Gopinathji Maharaj. Lord Swaminarayan had given him divine vision so that he may see Lord for His measurements even when He was many miles away.

Scriptures

During His time on earth Lord Swaminarayan aimed to write scriptures revealing the greatness of the Sampraday. In the short span of thirty-one years, Lord Swaminarayan created a series of scriptures that would not be possible for any normal individual to compose.

Fundamentally, scriptures of the Swaminarayan Sampraday are based on famous Hindu scriptures including the Vedas, and are not based on any radical principles. The content of all the scriptures by Lord Swaminarayan is based on the subject of religion, humanity, honesty, non-violence and mercy to mankind.

The scriptures written are easy to understand unlike other Hindu scriptures. The scriptures written are either in Sanskrit or Gujarati. Any scripture should be revered and it should be studied on a regular basis, to enable a saint or devotee to acquire the knowledge therein. Through acquiring knowledge and appreciating the divine personality of Lord Swaminarayan, a devotee is able to grow in his love for God.

Shikshapatri

> *"All My followers shall daily read this Shikshapatri. Those who cannot read shall listen to it with respect. When a reader of Shikshapatri is not readily available they shall worship it daily. All followers shall honour My word as My image with deep reverence."*
>
> *(Shikshapatri Sloka 208-209)*

The literal meaning of Shikshapatri is the 'letter of teachings'. Lord Swaminarayan was highly educated in the important scriptures of Hinduism at a very young age. His father, Dharmadev, personally taught Him.

Lord Swaminarayan selected key points of importance from these scriptures and made a small 'gutko' booklet. Eventually, this gutko formed the basis of the Shikshapatri that Lord wrote. It comprises of 212 slokas and was written in Vadtal on the 5th day of the bright half of the month of Maha VS 1882, on Vasant Panchmi.

It is the most accessible of religious texts because of its size, scope and relevance to everyday life. Lord Himself wrote the Shikshapatri in Sanskrit. It was then translated into other languages including Gujarati and subsequently into English.

If one abides by the Shikshapatri it improve the lives of individuals in this life and the next. They shall also shall attain the four objects in life being, dharma, artha, kama and moksha.

Lord wrote the Shikshapatri from His heart, by His own hand. It is a code of conduct for the benefit of all mankind. Lord has stated that the Shikshapatri is the perceptible form of Himself.

Shreemad Satsangijeevan

Shreemad Satsangijeevan is the core scripture of the Swaminarayan Sampraday. This divine scripture describes the life of Lord Swaminarayan for all the period He spent on Earth. It was prepared in order to enlighten devotees of the divine personality of Lord Swaminarayan. It covers the philosophy, spiritual wisdom, devotion and non-attachment of worldly objects of Lord Swaminarayan.

Shatanand Swami wrote the scripture, through the divine inspiration and request of Lord. Shatanand Swami compiled the scripture sitting next to Lord. Lord would read each chapter and comment on the supremacy of the literary piece created. The scripture written in Sanskrit contains 319 chapters. On the completion of the Shreemad Satsangijeevan, Lord took it on His head in an act of joy.

When Lord took departure from the earth in Gadhada, saints and devotees became inconsolable and extreme sadness filled the air. It was at this point that this great scripture was recited. It kindled the fond memories of Almighty God Supreme in the hearts of saints and devotees.

Vachnamrit

Vachnamrit is the nectar of all the spiritual and philosophical knowledge extracted by Lord Swaminarayan from all the Hindu scriptures for easy understanding for the satsangis.

It contains all the spiritual and philosophical understanding of questions asked by the saints and other devotees, and the replies given by Lord Swaminarayan. Many a time, Lord has asked the questions and He has also answered them. The questions relate to cosmic evolution, welfare of mankind and ultimate salvation.

The answers given by Lord Swaminarayan are given in simple language, so that even illiterate people can understand them easily.

In each and every Vachnamrit, the day of the fortnight, the month, the time, the year and the place where each sabha is held is stated. A clear description is given about Lord's appearance that day, His clothing, ornaments, garlands put on by the Lord, the direction of His face and the name of the main members in the assembly are described in the first paragraph.

This proves that the Lord was present when the questions were actually asked and answered, they were factual and not imaginary or created by someone. The name of the person asking the question is also mentioned in each of the Vachnamrits.

The great saints Shukanand Swami, Muktanand Swami, Gopalanand Swami, Brahmanand Swami and Nityanand Swami heard, collected and compiled the original words of Lord Swaminarayan and got them authenticated by Him. These Vachnamrits were thousands in number, but our Lord has selected only 273.

Vachnamrit is the main scripture of our sampraday and we have an immense amount to learn from it. If anybody reads them attentively, they need not read any other scripture for their ultimate salvation. The Vachnamrit is held in such high regard that discourses from it are recited daily in all Swaminarayan temples.

Bhaktachintamani

This scripture was composed by Nishkulanand Swami in poetic form, under the divine guidance of Lord Swaminarayan. It describes the activities of Lord Swaminarayan during His lifetime. The Bhaktachintamani is aimed to bring peace and upliftment to the souls of satsangis. Events and festivals that occurred during the lifetime of Lord Swaminarayan have been mentioned in some detail within the literature.

ShreeHari Digvijay

This scripture consists of 49 chapters. Nityanand Swami under the order of Lord Swaminarayan composed ShreeHari Digvijay. This scripture describes and proves that Lord Swaminarayan was Almighty God Supreme, through numerous discussions and debates.

Prominent Saints

Ramanand Swami - Guru of Lord Swaminarayan

Ramanand Swami was born in VS 1795 in Ayodhya under the name of Ramsharma into a Brahmin family. He was the incarnation of Uddhavji, Ramanuj Acharya initiated him in Shreerangkshetra, Tamil Nadu.

Ramanand Swami first met Nilkanth Varni in Piplana VS 1856. In VS 1857 Ramanand Swami initiated Nilkanth Varni with Bhagwati Mahadiksha. Subsequently in Jetpur in VS 1858 Ramanand Swami handed over his Acharyaship of the Sampraday to Sahajanand Swami, it was at this time that he granted two boons to Lord Swaminarayan.

Later that year in Faneni town he passed away urging his disciples to serve and obediently worship Lord Swaminarayan.

Muktanand Swami – Mother of Sampraday

Muktanand Swami was born as Mukunddas in VS 1814 in Amreli town (Saurastra) to parents Anandram and Radhadevi.

Once there was a very learned ascetic called Muldas and he took in a poor disowned pregnant woman called Ratanbai. She gave birth to a girl named Radhabai, in time she married a man called Anandram. Their first-born was Mukunddas. Mukunddas stayed celibate and wanted to leave to become a sadhu.

He was married but was not happy. Mukunddas played dumb to make his parents feel that it would be all right to let him go but his parents still tried many things to cure him but none worked. His parents and friends were becoming frustrated and fed up, finally Mukunddas decided it was the right time to leave and so he left.

He obtained diksha from Ramanand Swami on Vasant Panchmi VS 1842. He became a renowned poet and wrote Muktanand Kavya. His first meeting with Nilkanth Varni was in Loj VS 1856 where he was asked to give the meanings of Jeeva, Ishwar, Maya, Brahm and Parbrahm. Muktanand Swami died in VS 1887.

Gopalanand Swami – Yogi Raj

Gopalanand Swami was born as Khusalbhatt in VS 1837 in Todla town near Idar. He was an Audichiya Brahmin, his father was Motiram Sharma and his mother was called Kusladevi.

He obtained diksha in VS 1864 in Vadodara. Lord Swaminarayan held Gopalanand Swami in very high regard and he was very learned in Ashtang yoga. When the Lord left His mortal body and returned to Akshardham He left responsibility for the Sampraday and the Acharyas in his hands.

Gopalanand Swami arranged for an idol of Kastabhanjan Hanumanji to be installed in Sarangpur in which he invested a large amount of divine power, which is still evident today.

If Gopalanand Swami was capable of instilling such powers in Hanumanji, one should appreciate and not under estimate the infinite power of his guru, Lord Swaminarayan. Gopalanand Swami died in VS 1908.

Brahmanand Swami – Kavi Raj

Brahmanand Swami was born in VS 1828 in Khan, a town in Rajasthan on Vasant Panchmi. His father was called Shambhudan Barot (Charan) and his mother was called Laluba.

He obtained diksha in VS 1860 in Gerita town, near Sidhpur. He was initially named Shreerangdasji, later named Brahmanand and was also referred to as Brahmmuni. He was a very famous poet, had a jolly character and had a great bond of friendship with Lord Swaminarayan. He wrote the Brahmanand Kavya. He had skills in architecture and was tasked by the Lord to get land and money for building temples. He was involved in the construction of the temples at Vadtal, Junagadh and Muli.

The Lord had high respect for Brahmanand Swami and said anybody who sings 100 of his verses everyday would receive darshan of Almighty God Supreme. Brahmanand Swami died in Muli VS 1888.

Nityanand Swami - Pandit

Nityanand Swami was born as Dinmani Sharma in Dantia, a town near Lucknow in VS 1812. He was born into a Gaoud (Yajurvedi) Brahmin family. His father was called Vishnu Sharma and his mother was Virjadevi. He also had a brother called Govind Sharma.

He obtained diksha in Meghpur (Saurastra). Nityanand Swami was a very strong debater, he had a profound knowledge of all scriptures. He composed ShreeHari Digvijay and produced the first Gujarati translation of the Shikshapatri approved by Lord Swaminarayan. He died in VS 1908 in Vadtal.

Premanand Swami - Premsakhi

Premanand Swami was born as Hathiram in the town of Dora Bharuch in VS 1840. He was born to Hindu parents who abandoned him at a young age. A Muslim family raised him, his foster father was called Dosatai.

Dosatai was a good father and wanted Hathiram to learn the art of music. For this reason Dosatai sent Hathiram to

Vadodara to learn music. After some time, Lord Swaminarayan had arranged a musical concert, which Dosatai and Hathiram attended. This is where the affection and love between Hathiram and Lord Swaminarayan commenced. Thereafter Hathiram stayed with Lord.

Lord Swaminarayan gave Hathiram diksha and named him Nijbodhanand Swami. His name was later changed to Premanand, due to his extreme love for Lord. He was a born poet, many of his hymns are sung daily by devotees. Premanand Swami composed the words of the Chesta Pad, which is sung and recited daily at all Swaminarayan temples. He also wrote the Premanand Kavya. Premanand Swami died in VS 1911 in Gadhada.

Nishkulanand Swami – Vairagya Murti

Nishkulanand Swami was born as Lalji Suthar in VS 1822 in the town of Shekhpat, near Jamnagar. He came from a Gujar Suthar family. His father was Rambhai and his mother was called Amratbai.

He married Kankubai and had two sons named Govind and Madhavji. Nishkulanand Swami was strong in observance of penance and renunciation and non-attachment to worldly objects and pleasures. He had many other skills including carpentry, masonry and sculpting. Lord Swaminarayan personally asked Nishkulanand Swami to go and oversee the construction project of Dholera temple, when others were unwilling to go. He wrote Bhakta Chintamani and Nishkulanand Kavya (22 parts). He died in VS 1904 in Dholera.

Devanand Swami

Devanand Swami was born as Devidan in VS 1859 in Balol town near Dholka. His father was called Jijibhai and his mother was called Benjiba.

At a very young age, Ashutosh (Shankar) told him that he would one day meet God. He was also told that he would recognise God whilst God was licking ghee from His elbow. After seeing this feat at an age of around six he renounced worldly objects.

His initial diksha name was Abheydanand, then later changed to Devanand. He also was a poet and Brahmanand Swami was his guru. He wrote Devanand Kavya. He stayed as Mahant of Muli Temple for 22 years until his death in VS 1910.

Vasudevanand Brahmchari

Vasudevanand Brahmchari was born in VS 1855 in Malapur town in Gujarat. He was a Trivedi Movada Brahmin. He obtained diksha in Jetalpur and was initially named Gopalanand Brahmchari then later Vasudevanand.

Once at Loya village he was asked to do a katha by Lord. The assembly was overcome by his performance and Lord was very pleased. It was at this time the Lord gave him the new name of Vasudevanand Brahmchari. He wrote the Satsangi Bhushan and died in VS 1920 in Ahmedabad.

Shatanand Swami (Santdasji)

Santdasji was born in Meethila town in Nepal. His father was called Vishnudatt, who was a brahmin. He obtained diksha in Dabhan.

He had the gift of akhand samadhi, in which he could see Lord in divine form whatever he was doing, even during sleep. Many times he had remained in samadhi for six months at a time. At Gadhada the Lord asked him to compose Shreemad Satsangijeevan because of his power and divine vision. He has written many other scriptures and stotras including Shikshapatri Artha Dipika.

Bhumanand Swami

Bhumanand Swami was born as Rupjibhai in VS 1852 in a town called Keshiya near Jamnagar. His father was called Ramjibhai and his mother was called Kuverbai, his family name was Kadiya Rathod.

He was a sincere and devoted person and composed many kirtans about bhakti. He composed the Ghanshyam Leelamrut Sagaar scripture. He was persuaded by a friend to go to Gadhada to find the Lord. There he did meet the Lord and the scene is captured in the kirtan, 'Sarve sakhi jeevan jova ne chalo re ...'. After a four day fast he wrote the prominent 'thal' that is sung within the sampraday, 'Jamo thal jeevan jau vari...'. Bhumanand Swami died in VS 1924 in Manasa.

Shukanand Swami (Shuk Muni) – Personal Secretary of the Lord

Shukanand Swami was born as Jagannath in VS 1855 in Dabhan in Gujarat. He came from an Audichiya Brahmin family.

Through Lord's wish he obtained diksha from Muktanand Swami. He was referred to as the personal secretary of Lord. He wrote whatever the Lord wished. Lord Swaminarayan often called him His right arm. He wrote 16 scriptures, 7 in Sanskrit and 9 in Gujarati. He died in VS 1925 in Vadtal.

Gunatitanand Swami

Gunatitanand Swami was born as Mul Sharma in VS 1841, in the town of Bhadra in Gujarat. His father was called Bhodanath and his mother was called Sakarba. He always saw the divine image of the Lord. For about 40 years he stayed as Mahant at Junagadh Temple. He died in VS 1923 in Gondal.

Mulji Brahmchari – Lord's Ever Ready Attendant

Mulji Brahmchari was born in Machhiyav (Saurastra). He came from an Audichiya Brahmin family. He obtained diksha from Ramanand Swami.

Mulji Brahmchari was permanently by the side of Lord Swaminarayan, serving Him in every way. Mulji Brahmchari followed Lord wherever He went, in the same way a shadow follows a body. Mulji Brahmchari did not care about his personal well being, all his actions were for one purpose only, to please Lord Swaminarayan.

Once Lord asked Mulji Brahmchari for water. Mulji Brahmchari was seated on a high wall. Immediately he jumped from the high wall and gave Lord some water. Lord asked, "Why did you jump from such a high wall risking injury to yourself?" Mulji Brahmchari replied, "If I had not jumped I would have been late in your service, Lord."

Lord Swaminarayan often tested the strength of Mulji Brahmchari. Mulji Brahmchari was always firm and innocent and pure in his love and service for Lord. He died in VS 1904 in Gadhada.

Prominent Satsangis

Dadakhachar

Dadakhachar was a landowner in the Saurashtra region of Gujarat. Uttamsinh was his real name and Dadakhachar was his pet name. His father was Ebhelkhachar (also known as Abhaysinh). Dadakhachar had four sisters, Jaya, Lalita, Panchali and Nanu. The entire family were strong followers of Lord Swaminarayan. The main family residence was in Gadhada.

Lord Swaminarayan first came to Gadhada on VS 1861 by request of Ebhelkhachar. A strong bond of love developed between Lord Swaminarayan and Ebhelkhachar's family. Lord spent the greatest amount of time in Gadhada, in total 25 years. He treated the residence in Gadhada as His own. For these reasons Gadhada became a focal point in the sampraday.

When Ebhelkhachar left his mortal body for Akshardham, Dadakhachar became the sole owner of the entire estate. Lord tested Dadakhachar and his family members frequently, even though Lord realised that Dadakhachar and his family were strong devotees.

On one occasion, Lord asked Dadakhachar to leave the estate and take residence elsewhere. Dadakhachar did not hesitate for one moment, he immediately left following every command of Lord.

Once there was an assembly during the night. Lord commented to Dadakhachar, "It is bright at present just like daytime", Dadakhachar agreed with Lord even though it was dark, thinking that he could not see the light. Dadakhachar had total faith and trust in Lord. Dadakhachar was unique in the sampraday, in that he gave all he owned to Lord Swaminarayan and would always obey His every command.

Joban Pagi

Joban Pagi was a fierce villain, murderer and accomplished thief. He had no remorse in taking life. He had taken so many lives of Brahmins, such that he had a drum full of janois belonging to them. He came from Vadtal in Gujarat and just the mention of his name frightened people across the state of Gujarat.

At a large yagna performed by Lord in Dabhan, Joban attempted to steal Manaki, Lord's famous and divine horse. Joban wanted to test the divinity of Lord by stealing Manaki during the yagna. Joban tried to steal Manaki for three whole days, but whenever he tried to steal Manaki, Lord was ever present with Manaki at all times.

He realised the supremacy of Lord and asked for forgiveness. Lord Swaminarayan forgave Joban Pagi for his sins. From then onwards Joban Pagi became a strong devotee of Lord.

Such was his devotion to Lord that he collected dust, which had touched the divine feet of Lord Swaminarayan. He used to take a pinch of this dust with his daily meals. Once he had consumed all the dust he had, he fasted and ate no more for the remainder of his life.

Parvatbhai of Agatrai

Parvatbhai was a strong Kanbi devotee of Lord Swaminarayan. He was a person who had no attachment to his family members. He was a true example of how a jeeva should distinguish itself from the human body and its affairs, and how one should focus upon God.

Parvatbhai had only one son called Meghji. His son was very ill and had only a short time to live. Once Parvatbhai received a letter from Lord calling him to Gadhada. Parvatbhai left for Gadhada as soon as he received the letter. As he reached the edge of the village, a man from his village came to inform him that his son had died. Parvatbhai told the man to perform the funeral rites of his son. Parvatbhai continued his journey to Gadhada.

On reaching Gadhada, Lord asked Parvatbhai about his son. Parvatbhai replied, "My son is now very happy, experiencing complete bliss in Akshardham."

Parvatbhai was a man who understood that the only important thing in life is Lord. Parvatbhai realised that only devotion to Lord can release the jeeva from the cycle of birth and death. Parvatbhai had such faith in Lord Swaminarayan, that he could always visualise the divine murti of Lord at all times.

Ladhiba

Ladhiba was a widow from Bhuj and a disciple of Ramanand Swami. With time she became a strong devotee of Lord Swaminarayan. Ladhiba was much younger in age than Lord.

It is traditional for widows to wear simple and dark clothing. Lord tested Ladhiba on one occasion. Lord said to Ladhiba, "Ladhiba, put on rich and colourful garments and fetch water from the well." Ladhiba did not hesitate.

Whilst fetching water, ladies in the town asked, "At this old age whom have you married?" Ladhiba replied, "In this eternal universe, I have been born many times. I could not get an immortal husband, but now I have. I have found Lord Swaminarayan, He is my beloved 'husband' who will give me ultimate redemption and take me to Akshardham." On hearing this Lord was very pleased with Ladhiba.

Ladhiba was a person who could see Lord in all His glory even when He was many miles away. She was able to place other female devotees into samadhi and show them the divine abode of Akshardham. Lord Swaminarayan has described the supreme qualities of Ladhiba in the third Vachnamrit of Loya.

Jivuba

Jivuba was the daughter of Ebhelkhachar and the sister of Dadakhachar. She was an avatar of Laxmiji.

Jivuba first had darshan of Lord along with the rest of her family. Whenever Lord Swaminarayan held festivals, Jivuba would always be in the kitchen cooking and preparing fine foods for Lord.

On one occasion there was a disagreement in the construction of Vadtal temple, between Lord Swaminarayan and Brahmanand Swami, who had sent a letter to Lord. Jivuba was present while the Lord was preparing a reply to Brahmanand Swami. The Lord was advising Brahmanand Swami to construct a smaller temple. At this point Jivuba stated that a grand temple should be constructed in Vadtal. Lord Swaminarayan then said, "Laxmiji has spoken, so let it be."

Manaki Ghodi

Manaki Ghodi was the avatar of Garudji. She met Lord Swaminarayan when her servant, Jivendra, had come to take darshan of Lord in the village of Kariyana. Lord realised that the young Manaki Ghodi was beautiful and would be a proud owner of any king. To prevent Manaki Ghodi being taken away from Jivendra, Lord requested Jivendra to give Manaki Ghodi to Him, he agreed. Lord was extremely pleased and gave Jivendra His precious shawl (rheto) and money.

In describing Manaki

Ghodi's beauty, Premanand Swami, later said in a kirtan that of the many different breeds of horse, Kesar, Beri, Bodali, Fulmal, Tajan and Thiki, the Manaki breed was superior to all.

Lord Swaminarayan took great care of Manaki Ghodi and took great effort to train her. Over time Manaki Ghodi became inseparable from Lord. She would take Lord across Gujarat as He wished and forever remained with Him.

When Lord Swaminarayan left His mortal body and returned to Akshardham, Manaki Ghodi could not bear the pain and loss of Lord leaving her. Manaki Ghodi took no food or water after Lord's departure. Thirteen days after Lord's departure Manaki Ghodi left her mortal body and joined Lord in Akshardham.

Key teachings of Lord Swaminarayan

The five Panchvartman – Vows

Lord Swaminarayan stated that devotion and moral behaviour is essential for salvation and reaching divine Akshardham. A person must be pure in his actions and disciplined in life in order to be moral.

To help His followers maintain a high level of morality in life, Lord Swaminarayan defined five vows that His devotees must always observe. He stated that whoever wants to

embrace His sampraday must abide by these five vows:

- Abstain from drinking wine, liquor or any intoxicating drug
- Abstain from eating meat in any form
- Abstain from adultery
- Abstain from stealing even the smallest item
- Not to take food & drink from improper sources

These vows apply to all followers of the sampraday from acharyas, saints to householders. Such is the truth and purity of these vows that a person of any religion would benefit from observing these vows.

Ahimsa – non violence

> *"My disciples shall never intentionally kill any living creature, not even the smallest insects such as lice or bugs."*
> *(Shikshapatri Sloka 11)*

Ahimsa is a fundamental principle of Hinduism. This has been stated in the Vedas and all other great scriptures of Hinduism. Vedic law does not allow killing of living beings for food or sacrifice.

Control of life and death lies only at the hands of God. Only God has the power to create life and to take life away. Humans do not have the right to carry out the destruction of life. Lord Swaminarayan has categorically stated that His followers must not kill any living creature, whether it be for food or sacrificial purposes.

Blessing of God is best achieved by other acts of penance, Vedic ceremonies and rituals. There remains no reason to offer animals for sacrifice. Under the same fundamental reason, one must not accept meat even if it has been offered under sacrificial reasons.

Intoxication

One must not take any substances that will lead to the loss of self-control or that which over burdens the human mechanism. It is understood that the effect of taking intoxicating substances leads to deterioration in physical and mental health, lack of self-control and the uprising of wicked and evil actions.

> *"None shall ever eat meat, even if it be a offering in a sacrifice or shall ever drink liquor, drugs and intoxicating beverages even if it be offered to a deity."*
> *(Shikshapatri Sloka 15).*

Liquor, wine, intoxicating beverages, drugs are all intoxicating substances. Taking these substances in small quantities will inevitably lead to excessive quantities being taken through its addictive properties.

The intake of drugs to enhance spiritual belief is widespread but bears no sense. Drugs do not help in achieving salvation and an ideal saint or devotee does not take any intoxicant, since only control of ones senses and devotion to God will lead to salvation.

Taking onions and garlic is not permitted as they are regarded as being of tamas nature. Consuming tamas food such as onions and garlic leads to one's senses being aggravated and bad odour resulting. They make a person temperamental, angry and unable to control themselves.

Moksha – Salvation

> *"Jeeva dwells in the heart and is as minute as an atom. It is conscious and knowledgeable and by the virtues of its subjectivity, pervades the whole body. It is impenetrable, invisible, indivisible, indestructible and eternal."*
> *(Shikshapatri Sloka 105)*

The soul is immortal and is constantly going through the cycle of birth and death. It resides in the body of every living creature but is fundamentally separate from the body.

During the cycle of birth and death the soul suffers extreme and unbearable pain. The only opportunity for the soul to escape the cycle of birth and death through ones own action, is in the human form. This opportunity is not available in other life forms. If the chance is not taken whilst in human form then the soul must repeat its journey through the 8.4 million cycles of life and death.

For the jeeva to achieve ultimate moksha and attain eternal bliss, a devotee must abide by and follow the rules laid down by Lord Swaminarayan in the Shikshapatri. For greater detail refer to the final Vachnamrit of the last Gadhada Section.

Suicide

> *"None shall ever commit suicide, even in a place of pilgrimage or through anger or on some untoward action by taking poison, hanging, falling into a well, falling from a cliff edge or by any other means."*
>
> *(Shikshapatri Sloka 14)*

The jeeva can only attain salvation whilst in human form. Human life is rare and one must go through millions of births and deaths to achieve it. It is for this reason that suicide is deemed to be a useless waste of life.

It is through God's will, that one is given the human life form. On committing suicide, God will never give a second chance for salvation to a person that has taken their own life. The ultimate control of birth and death lies only with God and not with any human being. It is certain that the suffering increases in the next life for a person that has ended his or her own life.

The main reasons for suicide are sense of defeat, frustration, helplessness and failure. Any problem of any size or kind can be overcome through trust in God.

Suffering and pain are part of life and are dependent on

ones actions in their previous life, therefore one must accept and endure difficult times along with the good. Euthanasia, to assist in the early termination of life due to pain and suffering is forbidden, since only God has the power to control life and death.

Separate Assemblies

> *"My male and female disciples who come to the temple of Shree Krishna either daily or on days of religious festivals, shall keep themselves away from the opposite sex and after leaving the temple, they will behave as usual."*
>
> *(Shikshapatri Sloka 40)*

It is natural that males and females are attracted to each other. Frequent meetings and association between males and females results in greater attraction between them and finally it converts into lust or passion.

A devotee cannot remain focused on God whilst there is distraction in the form of the opposite sex. Even the most devout, highly spiritual yogis, sadhus and great persons have failed in their goal towards God due to such distraction.

It was for this reason that Lord Swaminarayan insisted on separate assemblies for the males and females. Females may attend the male assemblies but should sit separately from the males.

Lord Swaminarayan had constructed huge temples and installed idols of God. Ladies can go to the huge temples for darshan but the arrangement for darshan is separate from the males. This is to ensure that no male or female come into contact with each other during darshan.

Menstruation

The phenomenon of the menstrual cycle is completely natural. It is the path all women take in their lives towards motherhood.

> *"No woman shall touch anybody or any clothes etc. for three days during the period of menstruation, but can do so on the fourth day after taking a bath."*
> *(Shikshapatri Sloka 174)*

According to Swaminarayan religion, women, including the wives of the Acharya's, should never hide their menstruation periods. For the first three days and nights, they shall not touch anybody, any clothes or cook food. During the menstruation period, they should not even touch any women who are also in their menstruation.

If the menstruation starts before midnight then the day before midnight should be counted as the first day. If after midnight, then the day after midnight should be counted as the first day.

On the fourth day, after having a purifying bath, which includes washing her hair she should put on clean clothes. Then she should take nutritious food to gain energy. They can then return to normal household duties. If a woman herself cooks food on the fourth day, this should not be offered to God.

If a woman comes in to her period within 17 days, then she becomes pure by just having a bath. If on the 18th day she has to follow the rules for one night. If on the 19th day she has to follow the rules for two nights and if it is on the 20th day or after she has to follow the normal rules for menstruation.

Days after start of previous menstruation:

• Up to 17	Purified after having a full bath
• 18	Take bath after one day of observance
• 19	Take bath after two days of observance
• 20 or more	Full normal rules for menstruation

If women are in menstruation during their own wedding, personal holy festivals, any emergencies like riot and war, they are not forced to follow these rules. In such times of extreme hardship they may fast during these days.

If they touch any persons by mistake, then the sin can be atoned by observing fast on Rushi Pancham Vrata, which comes annually in the Hindu calendar on the 5th day of the bright half of the month of Bhadarvo.

The religious origin for observing the rules of menstruation dates back to ancient Vedic times and were devised by great Rishis, on the grounds that menstruation has impure implications. Separation and rest for the females during this period promotes well being and prevents additional complications arising.

The observance of menstruation rules prescribed is given direct reference in the Mahabharat, giving evidence of its importance, existence and relevance. The rules of menstruation for women are not unique to Hinduism, similar rules and obligations exist in Judaism, Christianity (Old Testament, Book of Levictus, Chapter 15) and Islam.

In modern society there are logical reasons for observing menstruation. The physical process of menstruation is regarded as unhygienic. Therefore, by avoiding contact with food, people and household items purity is maintained.

Throughout the month, women work hard looking after the home and family. During the period of menstruation the body is physically tired and painful. Lack of energy is also a symptom of menstruation. Therefore, by observing total rest, women are able to regain their strength.

Satsangi life

Kanthi

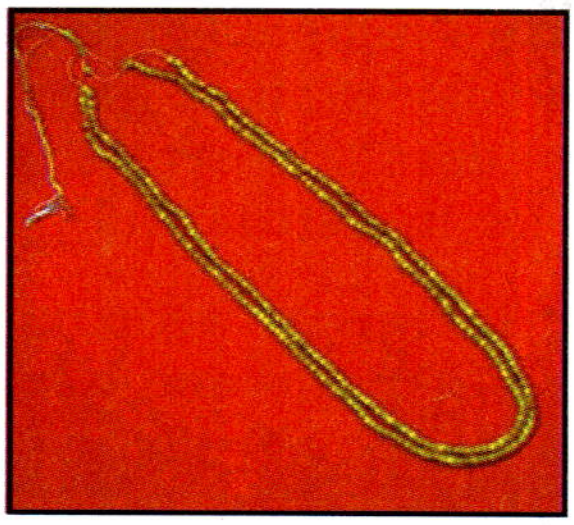

The kanthi is a double stranded necklace made of Tulsi. This is a significant symbol of our sampraday, and has been directly referred to by Lord Swaminarayan in the Shikshapatri.

The origin of the kanthi dates back to the time of Ramanand Swami and his guru Ramanuj Acharya. Ramanand Swami was the first to adorn a double stranded necklace made of Tulsi.

Parents of Lord Swaminarayan, also wore a kanthi, in the name of Lord Shree Krishna and Radha. Ramanand Swami had presented kanthis to them during a meeting in Prayagraj.

Lord has instructed His followers to wear a double stranded kanthi to symbolise Krishna and Radha. The length at which a person should wear a kanthi is also standardised to the level of the heart, the place in which God resides.

Tilak Chandlo

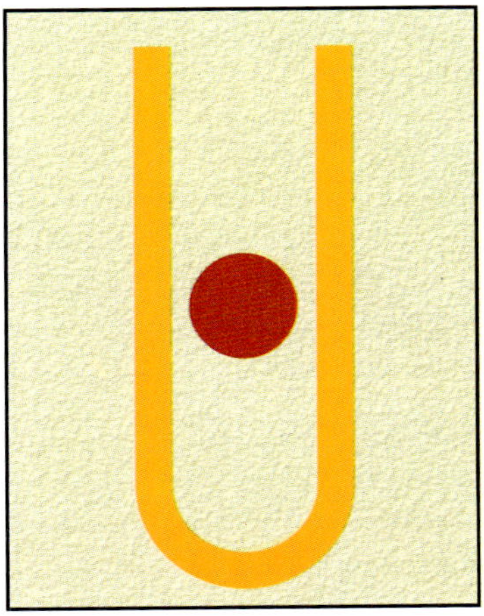

The tilak is the name of the 'U' shape and the chandlo is the circular dot between the tilak. The tilak is said to be Urdhva Pundra. Urdhva Pundra represents the shape of the lotus feet of Lord Swaminarayan.

The chandlo is made from red powder (kum kum or saffron), which symbolises Laxmiji (Goddess of Prosperity) living in the heart of Lord Swaminarayan.

The tilak is adorned by male satsangis on four parts of their body using Gopichandan (a yellow paste sanctified by the Gopis, which is found on the banks of the Lake Gopi in Dwarika). It is impressed on the forehead, chest and both the upper arms.

The forehead is the symbol of knowledge. The soul resides inside the heart. Almighty God Supreme resides in the soul, it is for this reason that a tilak is made on the chest. Our strength is characterised by the arms, thereby applying tilak on the arms utilises our strength in performing good deeds.

The benefit of having a tilak mark is of very great value. It protects you from worldly bondage, whilst maintaining the body as holy as the temple of God. It destroys any sins committed during the day. With out it, acts such as reciting the name of God, performing sacrificial fire and the study of scriptures are not accepted by God.

Mala

The mala is threaded with 108 beads and one larger bead. It is principally used as a counter whilst reciting the names of God. Almighty God Supreme has thousands of names, the main names are shortlisted into 108, and this is the reason for 108 beads.

The larger bead is regarded as the 'Mer' named after the divine Mount Meru. According to the scriptures the solar system revolves around Mount Meru. Therefore when doing Mala, when we reach the Mer, we touch it and return in the opposite direction but do not cross it.

When using the mala it is important to avoid touching the beads with the index finger as this is impure. The mala is veiled using a Gaumukhi, this avoids the mala touching the feet or ground and maintains purity.

Nitya Pooja

Nitya means daily and pooja is to worship God. Therefore pooja performed every day is known as Nitya Pooja.

The scriptures declare that the early hours of the morning are considered auspicious and the mind is more peaceful first thing than at any other time of the day. Devotees should do pooja at this time.

The satsangi should perform the calls of nature and then shower or bathe with clean water. While bathing one should remember Lord Swaminarayan. After bathing, devotees should cover themselves with one cloth on the upper body and another piece on the lower body. The clothes used for pooja should be fresh, clean and be kept separate from those worn during the day.

> *"All My disciples should get up daily before sunrise, offer prayers to Lord Shree Krishna and then go to answer the call of nature. Thereafter, sitting in one place they shall brush their teeth, bathe in clean water and then wear one washed cloth around the waist and one around the upper part of the body. Then they shall it in a clean place, on a suitable clean cloth, untouched by others, facing north or east and shall perform achaman."*
>
> *(Shikshapatri Slokas 49–51)*

For performing pooja, a devotee should sit on the floor (on a clean cloth), facing north or east. If possible, a silent environment is preferable.

Then one should perform achaman, sipping water using one's palm three times, which is a purifying act for the soul. Then one should apply tilak and chandlo as prescribed in the Shikshapatri.

> *"All males shall mark their forehead with a tilak having a chandlo in the centre. All married women shall make only a chandlo of kumkum on their forehead. Widows shall not mark their forehead with either tilak or chandlo. All My disciples shall then meditate upon Lord Shree Krishna and mentally offer Him sandalwood, flowers, etc."*
>
> *(Shikshapatri Slokas 52-53)*

The murti that should be in the pooja is that of Lord Swaminarayan, since He is Almighty God Supreme. A devotee should then perform manasi-pooja and then invite the Lord to take residence in the murti by recitation of the Ahavan mantra.

The devotee should then perform tapa-mala with arms raised, chanting the name of Lord whilst standing on the left leg and the right leg should be crossed over onto the left knee. Women should perform tapa mala whilst standing upright on both feet. Pradikshina of the murtis should then be performed whilst continuing to do mala. This is done by walking clockwise around the murtis taking darshan.

Then the Shikshapatri should be read. If one does not know how to read, then they should worship the Shikshapatri. Finally Lord returns to His abode by recitation of the Visarjan mantra.

Nitya Pooja brings devotees closer to Lord Swaminarayan. Lord Swaminarayan will stay with devotees at all times and provide guidance throughout the day.

Temple

Temple at Laxmiwadi - Gadhada, site of Lord's cremation

Lord Swaminarayan Himself stated that He resides in four places, temples, scriptures, acharyas and saints. The prime reason why one should attend temple is that Lord is ever present in the murtis at temples.

The atmosphere in the temple is calm, pure and sacred. There are fewer distractions in the temple, this enables one to worship peacefully and form a stronger bond with Lord Swaminarayan.

> *"All My followers shall go to temples of Lord Shree Krishna every evening and shall loudly sing kirtans in praise of Him and His qualities."*
> *(Shikshapatri Slokas 63)*

One should attend temple both morning and evening. However, during the day a person comes into contact with numerous evils and commits sins unknowingly. By going to temple in the evening one is able to wash these away by meditation of Almighty God Supreme.

A higher quality of worship can be performed in the temple, by taking part in kirtans, dhoon and katha. Therefore, the benefits and rewards are correspondingly higher, than if one is to perform bhakti at home.

One should not hesitate in attending temple to take darshan of Lord Swaminarayan. The human mind is fickle and therefore Lord Swaminarayan has stated in the Shikshapatri that one should take immediate action on acts of dharma, such as making donations to God.

Darshan

Darshan is a form of worship. It is a way of connecting a devotee to God and to gain His blessings. Regular and pious darshan leads to stronger belief and relationship with God.

When doing darshan one should be completely focused upon God. One should observe the beauty of His appearance and His charisma and over a period of time one should aim to transfix the image of God in one's heart and mind. Pure darshan will yield blessings and guidance from God Himself. Darshan should not be performed for any form of personal gain.

Males should do darshan lying down with seven parts of the body (eyes, forehead, mouth, hands, chest, knees and feet) touching the ground. The eighth and most important part, the mind, should be focused upon God. The hands should be crossed so that the right hand touches Gods right foot and the left hand touches the left foot. Darshan should be comprised of a minimum of 6 repetitions, the final darshan asking for forgiveness from Lord.

Females should perform darshan and dedicate themselves to God. They should touch their arms, head, eyes, mouth and mind to the floor in reverence to the lotus feet of Lord Swaminarayan.

"One shall never go empty handed to a guru, deity or a king. One shall never commit a breach of trust and shall never praise oneself."

(Shikshapatri Sloka 37)

When going for darshan of God one should not go empty handed. A small gift should always be offered to God whether it is fruit, flowers or money.

On approaching God one should bow with respect. By touching the images of God, the Lotus feet of Lord and Holy Scriptures, one gains direct blessings from God. This also gives peace and satisfaction to the soul.

Aarti

Aarti is a religious ceremony performed to gain darshan and blessing of God.

Aarti is conducted by the singing of a special prayer to God and also playing of musical instruments. Muktanand Swami composed the words to the aarti, he did this when realising that Lord Swaminarayan was Almighty God Supreme.

A ghee lamp is used in the aarti, to radiate pure light upon the murti of God. During the ceremony the ghee lamp is rotated in a circular manner to enable the devotees to have divine darshan of God, starting from the feet of Lord. The devotees must focus their mind upon God and observe His divine beauty.

The person performing the aarti must be physically and mentally pure and clean.

In shikharbandh mandirs aarti is performed five times a day. The five aartis are:

- Mangla aarti - performed before sunrise
- Shangar aarti - performed after God has adorned His clothes
- Rajbhog aarti - performed after the noon offering of food
- Sandhya aarti - performed at dusk before sunset
- Shayan aarti - performed before God rests for the night

In dev mandirs, aarti is performed in the morning and evening only.

Vandu and Chesta Pad

When Lord Swaminarayan was present on earth, the saints and satsangis of our sampraday were always with Him. Assemblies were held at many places and at all times of the day, from early morning to late in the night, as He desired.

The saints became used to having Lord Swaminarayan in their lives. Often when saints were sent to other towns away from the Lord, they truely missed His presence. When the Lord was present with the saints they were able to see with their own eyes His beauty, His form, His dress and His turban. They were able to talk to Him, how He was seated, the elegance of His walk, the way He slept, prepare food for Him and see the way He ate.

But once Lord had left His mortal body, the saints and satsangis could not bear the separation, words could not describe the pain and suffering that they were experiencing.

They had lost direction in their lives. They missed the Lord terribly, they found meditation difficult and the assemblies lacked focus.

The loss felt by the saints and devotees was infinite, thereby Gopalanand Swami requested Premanand Swami to compile the Chesta Pad after the Lord's departure, which vividly describes Lord Swaminarayan's daily routine and habits.

Premanand Swami compiles the Vandu Pad

For the purpose of meditation the Vandu Pad were complied by Premanand Swami on the 14th day of the dark half of the month of Maha VS 1880, during the presence of Lord

Swaminarayan. The Vandu Pad describes the beauty and appearance of Lord Swaminarayan.

The Vandu and Chesta Pads are a superb piece of poetry. It enabled saints and satsangis to focus their distressed minds on the divine murti of Lord Swaminarayan in all His glory and splendour. The tradition of reciting these Pads has remained an important part of the evening ceremony at temples of the Swaminarayan Sampraday.

Principal Hindu concepts and beliefs

This is a key concept of Hinduism, in that there is only one God. He has many attributes, forms and names. According to the Vedas, God is sakar, has a divine physical form, taking eternal residence in His heavenly abode.

> *"When evil dominates good, and righteous people are suffering, Lord Almighty incarnates Himself on earth in human form."*
>
> *(Shreemad Bhagwad Gita)*

For this reason there have been many avatars of God over time in human and animal form. Different avatars of God all ultimately lead to Almighty God Supreme. One should draw a clear distinction between avatars of God and Demi-Gods, which are in fact followers of God. Demi-Gods are controllers of the universe and its elements.

Reincarnation, Karma and Moksha

The principles of reincarnation, karma and moksha are fundamental to Hinduism.

The soul that resides in the body of the human is indivisible, indestructible and eternal. In human form the body acts as a carrier to the soul. When a person dies the soul enters a new body.

God determines the quality of one's next life based upon the karma undertaken in one's previous life. The soul yields the benefits and suffers the pain of the actions undertaken in one's past life. The soul is indestructible and continues the everlasting cycle of birth and death, which is associated with extreme pain.

The ultimate goal of the soul is to gain moksha and to reach the abode of Almighty God Supreme. This can only be achieved through devotion to God, pure karma and spiritual knowledge of the soul and God.

Ahimsa

Ahimsa means non-violence. Hindus must observe Ahimsa in their actions and mental attitude. It is the defining principle that society in general must observe Ahimsa if morality and dharma is to prevail amongst the subjects.

The moral of Ahimsa is evident in all major religions and societies. Mahatma Gandhi was the modern day leader to observe Ahimsa. He used Ahimsa in the struggle to gain freedom and independence from the British Raj.

Vegetarianism

All the prominent scriptures of Hinduism declare that all Hindus must have a pure vegetarian diet. God and great Rishis have preached vegetarianism throughout time, the reasons behind this are simple and are very relevant in today's society.

The code of a vegetarian diet stems directly from the principle of Ahimsa. In the eyes of God all forms of life are sacred and equal. God alone, is the creator of all forms of life. He alone creates and ceases life. Therefore, as humans we do not have the power nor the authority to take the life of another creature.

We must not consume meat under any circumstance, as this would involve killing another life. This principle also applies in situations of extreme starvation.

The consumption of eggs is prohibited. Life commences in the form of an egg and therefore consumption of eggs is also deemed to be the taking of a life, since one will be partaking in ceasing a life in its infancy.

In Hindu society, the cow is regarded as pious and sacred. Certain sections of the Hindu communities accept that taking beef is a sin, but it is acceptable to eat other forms of meat. This view abuses the principles of Hinduism for ones own advantage. No form of meat is allowed throughout Hinduism, there are no deviations from this rule at any point.

It is not only the meat eater that is committing a great sin. All those involved in the chain, from the farmer to the meat eater are equally to blame in the eyes of God. The Shikshapatri Bhashya (sloka 15), based on the teachings of Manu Rishi, the first law giver to mankind, defines those who equally sin by partaking in the process of meat consumption. The following individuals are defying this fundamental principle of vegetarianism; one that condones meat eating, slaughterer, butcher, seller, buyer, cook, distributor and eater.

The thought and actions of a person are directly linked to food consumed. Meat is classed as a bad type of food. Eating meat will give rise to bad thoughts and actions. Pure thoughts and actions can be achieved only through observing a strict vegetarian diet. It is said that those who consume meat are of demonic form.

In western society more and more people are opting to choose vegetarianism as a way forward. The risks and dangers of consuming meat products are rife, recent examples of BSE, CJD and Salmonella highlight this point. Eating meat is a health risk to ones own life.

Contrary to what people say, the human body is not designed to consume meat and we can acquire all the nutrients, vitamins and minerals required for a healthy life through a pure vegetarian diet. In fact, one is likely to lead a more healthy life being vegetarian.

Respect for parents, ancestors and teachers

> *"All My followers during their lifetime shall serve their parents, gurus, and those who are in pain according to their ability."*
> *(Shikshapatri Sloka 139)*

Hindus are raised on the ideology that parents are on an equal par to God. For this reason it is common in Hinduism for children to touch the feet of their parents and elders. The service and well being of parents is the sole responsibility of the children. This duty is divine and pious. It is regarded sinful not to take care for one's parents.

Gurus and teachers are respected for the influence they have on one's life, since they impart education, experience and knowledge to a pupil.

Hindu Caste System

The creation of the Hindu caste system dates back to the Vedic era. According to the Vedas, human society was created from different parts of God, Vairat Narayan.

These four social classes, Brahmin, Kshatriya, Vaishiya, and Shudra are the castes of Hinduism known as Varnas.

> *"Brahmins shall have virtues such as tranquillity, self restrain, forgiveness and contentment. My Kshatriya devotees (Warrior caste) shall have bravery, patience and similar qualities. The Vaishiya caste shall practise farming, trading and banking. The Sudhra caste shall serve the above mentioned three castes."*
> *(Shikshapatri Sloka 89-90)*

The common roles adopted by each caste are as follows, Brahmins being priests and teachers, Kshatriyas being warriors and rulers, Vaishiyas being merchants and farmers and Shudras being servants.

The caste system was devised in the Vedic period, to distribute social and employment duties and to create a community structure.

Sanskars

Hinduism has defined the concepts of sanskars. The sanskars are ceremonial acts that define the different stages of ones life from conception to death. There are sixteen sanskars in total, each providing unique direction in life. The sanskars are performed by way of religious ceremonies and ritual acts that lend purification and development of the body and mind. One can only be Hindu if these sanskars are followed according to Vedic law.

A brief description is detailed below:

1	Garbhadhan	Act of conception according to prescribed rules.
2	Punsavan	Performed in early pregnancy.
3	Simantonnayan	Performed in late pregnancy.
4	Jaatkarma	Performed at birth to welcome the child to the world. It involves whispering the name of God to the child and placing a small amount of honey or jaggery in the child's mouth.
5	Naamkaran	Naming ceremony of the newborn child performed on the eleventh day. The name given to the child is associated to the date and time of birth.
6	Nishkarma	At the age of four months the child is exposed to the elements of nature.
7	Annaprashan	The baby is given solid foods at the point of teething.
8	Chaulkarma	This ceremony involves the initial shaving of the child's head. This is performed between the age of one and three.

9	Karnvedh	The child's ears are pierced.
10	Upnayan	Yagnopavit ceremony where a janoi is adorned at the age of eight.
11	Vedarambh	A mantra of God is explained to the child when education begins. This prayer aims to instil intelligence in the young child.
12	Samavartan	Graduation ceremony is performed on completion of studies.
13	Snatak	Bathing ceremony at home on completion of studies.
14	Vivaha	Marriage, the second stage of life. A lifelong partnership between a man and a woman is formed. The duties and responsibilities are explained and assigned to husband and wife.
15	Agniparigraha	Pooja is performed daily to Agni Dev brought home from the wedding ceremony.
16	Tretagnisangraha	Death rites. The soul is immortal and leaves behind the body. The fire brought home from the wedding ceremony is used to cremate the body, returning the body to its five elements being earth, water, fire, air and space.

Sutak – Days of impurity

On the birth or death of a relative, one has to undergo a period of sutak, which commences from the birth or death of the relative. One must take a purifying bath on hearing the death of a relative. A person who has sutak should not perform religious acts such as pooja, preparing food for Lord and aarti.

"All My followers shall observe the days of impurity (sutak) after the birth and death of a relative according to the closeness of their relationship and as prescribed for them in the scriptures."

(Shikshapatri Sloka 88)

On the birth of a child, the father and relatives within 7 generations must undergo sutak for 10 days. Relatives within 8 to 14 generations should observe 3 days of sutak. The mother of the new born child should observe sutak for 31 days on the birth of a boy and 41 days on the birth of a girl.

On the death of a relative, 7 generations must undergo sutak for 10 days. Relatives within 8 to 14 generations should observe 3 days of sutak.

Eclipse

An eclipse occurs when the moon or the earth obstructs the light of the sun reaching the earth or moon respectively. According to Hindu scriptures the phenomena of the eclipse occurs because of the demon Rahu. The period preceding the eclipse and that during the eclipse is deemed to be impure, as the evil forces of Rahu prevail at the time of the eclipse.

> *"Whenever a solar or a lunar eclipse takes place, all My satsangis shall immediately suspend all work and after purifying themselves, by means of a bath, shall chant the mantra of Lord Shree Krishna. When the eclipse is over all shall take a bath with their clothes on. Thereafter, householders shall give alms to the poor, according to their means and other shall worship Lord Shree Krishna."*
>
> *(Shikshapatri Sloka 86-87)*

Lord Swaminarayan states that satsangis should perform additional penance and acts of devotion during an eclipse. One should not eat 9 hours before a lunar eclipse and 12 hours before a solar eclipse. During an eclipse water and food containing water should be discarded. On the completion of an eclipse one must take a full bath, perform pooja and be charitable in their actions.

The Sacred Cow

The sacred cow is said to be the embodiment of the Demi-Gods. Images of her often show different Demi-Gods residing in different parts of her body.

In Hinduism, the cow is deemed to be one of the most precious gifts that can be given in a religious ceremony. In the Vedic age the cow was a real blessing to the rural community.

Hindu society has domesticated the cow over time and all of mankind has become dependent on the cow for milk. All products yielded by cows are deemed to be pure and are used in religious ceremonies. The cow's dung is used for fuel and mixed with mud as a plastering for walls and floors.

It is not surprising that the cow has high respect in Hindu society and is often referred to as 'gao maata'.

Swastik

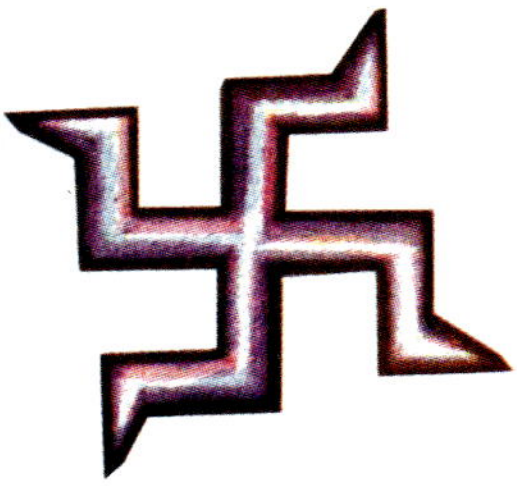

The Swastik has been used as an auspicious symbol in Hinduism over time in defending righteousness and overcoming evil forces.

The Swastik of Hinduism is a religious symbol and must not be confused with the Nazi Swastik.

Aum

In Hinduism, Aum is the name and symbol of the God and is used in prayers since it is considered to carry great divine powers. It is considered to be the essence of all great scriptures, including the Vedas.

Aum is the origin of Sanskrit and all languages as it was the first word to be spoken. Aum is in the shape of the number '3'. This represents the Trinity, Brahma, Vishnu and Shiva. Above the three is a half moon and the dot, which represents the momentary silence between two successive chants. By pronouncing Aum a full range of sounds and the entire phenomenon of sound is created.

The chanting of this mantra has a unique effect on the human mind, by giving inner peace to one that chants the mantra.

Ganga – River Ganges

Hindus regard the Ganga as the holiest river in the world. It flows from the mountains of the Himalayas. The water of the Ganga is believed to be holy because it liberates the soul from sins, and was blessed by Lord Vaman, who touched the water of Ganga by His feet.

King Bhagirath wanted to liberate the souls of his ancestors. This could only be done by the flow of the Ganges. But the Ganges was in the heavens. King Bhagirath performed penance to impress Ganga. Ganga came to earth by flowing through the hair of Lord Shiva, so as not to smash the earth on her descent.

There are many pilgrimage sites, but the holiest sites are at Haridwar and Rishikesh, which are in the foothills of the Himalayas. Kashi (Varanasi) is a holy city along the banks of the Ganga.

Gods

Lord Ram

Lord Ram was born in Ayodhya in Uttar Pradesh region of India. Lord Ram incarnated on earth hundreds of thousands of years ago, during the treta yug. He was born at midday, on the 9th day of the bright half of the month of Chaitra.

Lord Ram was born to King Dasaratha and Queen

Kaushaliya. King Dasaratha was married to three Queens, Kaushaliya mother of Lord Ram, Kaikai mother of Bharat and Sumitra mother of Laxman and Shatrughna. Lord Ram was the eldest brother.

The reason for the incarnation of Lord Ram was to kill the demon Ravana, who was causing havoc and distress to society. The conquest of Ravana re-established peace, righteousness and harmony on earth.

Lord Ram was married to Sita, the daughter of King Janaka. When offering his daughter in marriage, King Janaka had invited many kings and princes from far off places to his palace. Janaka had offered the hand of his daughter to the Prince that would break the mighty bow of Lord Shiva. Many Princes failed including the demon Ravana. Only Lord Ram was able to break the mighty bow of Lord Shiva and thus became Sita's bridegroom.

The great epic Ramayan tells the life story of Lord Ram.

Lord Krishna

Lord Krishna was born in Mathura in Uttar Pradesh region of India, at midnight, on the 8th day of the dark half of the month of Shravan approximately 5000 years ago.

Lord Krishna was born to Vasudev and Devaki. One of the main reasons was for Lord Krishna to kill the evil demon Kans, His mama.

Kans had known that his destroyer would be the eighth child born to his sister. Kans had imprisoned Vasudev and Devaki, and had killed all seven children born to Devaki. On the birth of their eighth child, Lord Krishna, Vasudev miraculously escaped from jail and went to Gokul. Here he exchanged the newborn Lord Krishna with

Yogamaya, daughter of Yasoda and Nand and returned to jail.

Kans found out that the eighth child had been born to Devaki and tried to kill Yogamaya, but she escaped. Kans did not know that Lord Krishna had taken birth and was safe with Yasoda in Gokul.

Lord Krishna grew up in Gokul living with Yasoda and Nand. He was surrounded by thousands of devotees, Gopis and friends. At a young age Lord Krishna had a personal fondness of the flute, admiration of cows and the taste of curd. Lord Krishna is often depicted in a blue complexion for artistic purposes, but actually had a dark complexion, hence the name Shyam.

On growing up He left for Mathura where He killed Kans in battle in the Dhanush Yagna. Lord Krishna then left Mathura and went to Dwarika in Gujarat with His followers.

During His life He had thousands of beloved Gopis, but Radha was His true consort. Lord Krishna played a vital part in the Mahabharat, being the personal charioteer of Arjun where, along with the other Pandav brothers, He defeated the evil Prince Duryodhan and his brothers.

Lord NarNarayan

There was once a demonic man called Kunchi who did penance upon Lord Brahma and pleased Him. As a result Lord Brahma gifted Kunchi a boon. Kunchi first requested to live forever, but was denied this request because even Lord Brahma could not live forever. So Kunchi requested to have 1000 protective shields. He would lose one shield, when one being had completed penance for 1000 years and then fought Kunchi for another 1000 years. In order to take away all of Kunchi's protective shields and kill him, one would have to continuously repeat the cycle of penance and fighting.

Knowing that he was invincible, he became selfish and wanted to rule the world. All the Demi-Gods pleaded to Lord Vishnu to help resolve the situation. To resolve the problem, Lord Vishnu reincarnated Himself into two separate beings, these being Lord Nar and Lord Narayan.

Lord Nar and Lord Narayan were born to Dharmadev and Murtidevi, but were born as young men (they had no childhood) at Narayan Ghat along the banks of the Sabarmati River in Ahmedabad.

As soon as they were born, Lord Narayan started penance for 1000 years and then went to fight Kunchi for 1000 years. Whilst Lord Narayan was fighting Kunchi, Lord Nar started His Penance. After Lord Narayan had fought for 1000 years, Lord Nar went to fight Kunchi and Lord Narayan started another 1000 years of penance.

This continued until Kunchi was left with one final protective shield. At this point Kunchi realised that if he continued to fight he would be killed, so retreated to Lord Surya and begged for protection. Lord Nar went to fight Kunchi, as it was His turn to fight him, but could not get to him as Lord Surya protected him. As a result Lord Nar and Lord Narayan went back to their heavenly abode, Badrikashram.

Many centuries later Kunchi reincarnated as Karna, the son of Kuntaji. But because Karna still had one gifted life left from his previous incarnation as Kunchi, he was born with a protective shield. In order to kill Karna, this shield had to be removed. Lord Narayan was incarnated as Lord Krishna and Lord Nar was incarnated as Arjun. As it was the turn of Lord Nar to fight Kunchi, Arjun was the one that killed Karna. This is illustrated in the epic Mahabharat.

Demi-Gods

Trimurti

God can be seen in many different incarnations, but this one God has three main representations. Brahma, the Creator, Vishnu, the Preserver and Shiva, the Destroyer.

Brahma

Brahma is the Creator in the sense that he creates the world and its beings to exist. Brahma's consort is Savitri and Sarasvati, the Goddess of learning and music is his daughter. Brahma rides on Hansa, a swan. In Indian art, Brahma is represented with four faces, one looking to each of the points of the compass. These faces represent the four Vedas or books of sacred hymns.

Vishnu

Vishnu is the preserver. He behaves as a lawful, devout Hindu, and protects and sustains all that is good in the world. Vishnu's vehicle is the half-man half-eagle known as Garuda. Vishnu's consort is the beautiful Laxmi who came from the sea and is the Goddess of Wealth. She is often represented sitting on a lotus flower.

Shiva

Shiva is the deity of death and destruction, without which growth and rebirth could not take place. Shiva has a third eye on the centre of his forehead, opens only when he is extremely angry and has destructive powers. His matted hair carries the Goddess Ganga down to earth. Shiva is often worshipped in the form of lingam, a black stone. Shiva's consort is Parvati, daughter of the Himalayas.

Ganesh

Ganesh is the son of Lord Shiva and Goddess Parvati. When Lord Shiva left home and went to the remote peak of Mount Kailash, he left behind his wife Parvati. He sat for many years in deep meditation and at home Parvati was depressed in the absence of Lord Shiva.

To fill the missing companionship of Shiva, Parvati with the will of Lord Shiva created a son with the qualities of both parents. This child was named Ganesh. However, Lord Shiva was not aware of the existence of Ganesh.

When Lord Shiva at last returned from Mount Kailash, he found himself barred from his own home by an unknown boy claiming to be the son of Parvati. Ganesh had been told by Parvati not to let anyone into the house whilst she was bathing. A quarrel began between Lord Shiva and Ganesh, which eventually ended with Lord Shiva chopping Ganesh's head off, which travelled into distant space.

Lord Shiva told Parvati what he had done and realised that the boy he killed was actually his son. In grief, he ordered his attendants to bring the head of the first living creature they saw. Obeying Lord Shiva's commandment they returned with the head of an elephant. Taking the head, Lord Shiva placed it on to the body of Ganesh and brought him back to life.

Parvati did not like the appearance of Ganesh, now with the elephant head, and was annoyed with Lord Shiva. In remorse, Lord Shiva gave Ganesh blessings that he will be worshipped first in any ceremony that will be undertaken from now on.

Ganesh has great spiritual significance for Hindus. He is considered to be a remover of obstacles and represents wisdom and perfection. We worship Ganesh before commencing any new chapter in life, bringing good luck and defeating evil.

Hanuman

Sarangpur Hanumanji

Hanuman is the son of the Vaayu, Wind God and his mother was Anjni. He was the Chief Commander of King Sugreeva's army. Hanuman is a celibate brahmin and is learned in yoga, medicine and the Vedas.

Hanuman is in the form of a monkey, representing the Hindu concept that animal are also God's creation. He possesses enormous strength, valour and courage.

Hanuman is the ever present and single-minded servant of God. He served Lord Ram in the conquest to overcome and kill the demon Ravana. Today,

Hanuman is revered throughout Hinduism for his strength, courage and ardent devotion to Almighty God Supreme. Dharmadev, father of Lord Swaminarayan, revered Hanuman. Hanuman came to help Lord Swaminarayan and His family on numerous occasions.

Prominent Hindu Scriptures

Mahabharat

The great epic of the Mahabharat is deemed to be the longest poem in existence. It was compiled thousands of years ago by Vyas Muni.

The central plot in the Mahabharat concerns the Pandavas (spirit of good) and the Kauravas (spirit of evil) and the battle fought in Kurukshetra. It covers code of life, philosophy of social and ethical relations, personal and family issues.

Ramayan

Ramayan is the great epic in Sanskrit that tells the factual story of Lord Ram, His wife Sita, Laxman, Bharat, Hanuman against the evil forces of Ravana, centred on the city of Ayodhya, birthplace of Lord Ram. The epic depicts Lord Ram's exile to the forest for fourteen years, His defeat of Ravana and His re-establishment as King of Ayodhya after His return from exile. The story centres on the moral behaviour of family relationships.

The Ramayan is a source of guidance, inspiration and morality of Hindu life. Valmiki originally wrote the Ramayan in Sanskrit.

Shreemad Bhagwad Gita

Shreemad Bhagwad Gita is contained within the Mahabharat and comprises 18 chapters and 700 slokas.

During the battle between the Pandavas and the Kauravas, Lord Shree Krishna fought on the side of Pandavas, being the spirit of good as the personal charioteer of Arjun. When the battle between the Pandavas and the Kauravas commenced, Arjun could not bear to commence battle against the Kauravas, his close relatives that were opposing him. Shree Krishna then reminded Arjun of his duty and gave him divine advice. The words of wisdom and advice of Shree Krishna to Arjun are known as the Shreemad Bhagwad Gita. The main aim of the Gita is to uphold one's duty in life.

Shreemad Bhagwat

Shreemad Bhagwat contains stories of incarnations of God and great kings and sages of the past. It also gives detailed knowledge about the universe. Shreemad Bhagwat consists of twelve chapters. During his time on earth the great sage Vyas Dev recorded the spiritual pastimes of Lord Shree Krishna in the ancient Vedic literatures.

Lord Swaminarayan has given particular attention to the fifth and tenth chapters. The fifth chapter describes the way in which one should mediate upon Lord and the tenth chapter describes the divine glory and pastimes of Lord Shree Krishna.

The Vedas

The Vedas are deemed to be the first books known to mankind. Originally, God communicated the Vedas through word of mouth. The holy Vedas are eternal, the knowledge was revealed to the great thinkers.

There are four Vedas, namely Rug-Veda (deals with general knowledge), Yajur-Veda (deals with knowledge of Karma), Sam-Veda (deals with worship) and Atharva-Veda (deals with knowledge of science).

Festivals

Swaminarayan Jayanti, Ramnavmi

Ramnavmi is the birthday of Lord Swaminarayan and Lord Ram, on the 9th day of the bright half of the month of Chaitra. Lord Swaminarayan was born at 10:10pm and Lord Ram at midday.

This day is very pious for the Swaminarayan Sampraday, marking the arrival of Almighty God Supreme on this earth. On this day, fasting is observed by devotees to ensure that their mind is fixed upon God. Everyone must attend temple to take the divine darshan of God on His birthday. On this day Lord is swayed on a decorated cradle.

Janmashtami

Janmashtami is the birthday of Lord Shree Krishna and falls on the 8th day of the dark half of the month of Shravan. The birth of Lord Shree Krishna is celebrated at midnight, the time He was born.

On this day fasting is observed by devotees to ensure that their minds are fixed upon God. Temples throughout the world celebrate the birth in a grand manner and also by chanting the name of Lord Krishna. On this day Lord is swayed on a decorated cradle.

NarNarayan Jayanti

Lord Nar and Lord Narayan were born to Dharmadev and Murtidevi, but they were born as young men, having no childhood. NarNarayan Jayanti is celebrated to commemorate the birthday of Lord NarNarayan on Falgun

Nakshetra, which is based on the solar calendar. On this day deities come to earth and sway NarNarayan on a swing decorated with flowers.

On this day satsangis go and pray at the temple to gain blessings and pay respect to Lord NarNarayan on His auspicious birthday.

Maha Shivratri

The festival of Maha Shivratri is celebrated on the 14th day of the dark fortnight of the month of Maha. The day signifies the birth date of Lord Shiva, during this day satsangis observe fast and go to temples to worship and celebrate the festival.

Devotees perform pooja to the Shivalinga by bathing it with milk, ghee and honey and other scented perfumes.

Vaman Jayanti

Lord Vaman was an incarnation of Vishnu. He took incarnation in the form of a dwarf, to regain control for the deities and defeat the demon Baliraja.

The festival of Vaman Jayanti celebrates the birth of Lord Vaman on the 12th day of the bright half of the month of Bhadarvo.

Ganesh Choth

Ganapati dev's birthday is celebrated on the 4th day of the bright half of the month of Bhadarvo. Blessings are always taken from Ganesh when commencing any new event in one's life, whether it be an opening of a new business or attending the first day at school.

Ekadashi

We all abide Ekadashi every fortnight, but most of us do not yet know the story behind Ekadashi. Ekadashi arrives on the eleventh day of each lunar cycle. Each lunar month has two cycles a bright and a dark half, hence there are two Ekadashis each month and 24 in a year.

Ekadashi is defined as E-KA-DASHI – which simply means *one plus ten*. On this day the main aim is to control all our ten senses; hearing, touch, sight, taste, smell, speech, actions of arms and legs, natural bodily functions, sexual desire and the eleventh, the mind.

The story of Ekadashi originated before the time of Lord Swaminarayan. Ekadashi was actually the name of a lady.

Nadijung had a demon son called Murdanav. Murdanav wanted to live forever, and to gain such a boon he did penance to impress Lord Brahma. He impressed Lord Brahma and asked that he should live forever. Lord Brahma could not give the demon such a powerful boon, but he said that only a woman could kill Murdanav.

Murdanav, with his new found power began to harass and distress people and deities. The deities along with the people and Lord Brahma went to Lord Vishnu, to explain their troubles inflicted upon them by Murdanav.

Lord Vishnu, Lord Brahma and other deities battled with Murdanav, but nobody could kill him due to the boon granted by Lord Brahma. After some time Lord Vishnu took rest in the caves in the Himalayas, but Murdanav followed Lord Vishnu to the caves. From the ten senses and the mind of Lord Vishnu, a beautiful lady arose.

When Murdanav saw this beautiful lady, he instantly fell in love with her. Murdanav asked the lady to marry him. In reply, the lady said that she would marry Murdanav on one condition, that he would have to defeat her in battle to death. In Murdanav's obsession to marry this beautiful lady he did not realise that during the battle one of them would die. Since the lady had the strength of Lord Vishnu, Murdanav was killed in battle.

Lord Vishnu was very grateful and granted the lady a wish. The lady said that she wanted her name to be recognised in years and centuries to come. Lord granted her this wish and named a day after her, Ekadashi, and stated that all mankind should observe penance on this day, by controlling their senses and mind.

"All My followers shall observe self discipline on Ekadashi, Janmashtami and birth anniversaries of other deities, Shivratri, etc. and celebrate them with great reverence and festivity. If one is fasting on the day of self discipline, one shall make every effort to avoid sleeping during the day time, as this nullifies the fast, just as sexual indulgence does."
(Shikshapatri Sloka 79-80)

On Ekadashi we are supposed to fast. A complete fast is one where you fast all day on Ekadashi and do ek-tanu (eat once a day), on days before and after Ekadashi. By fasting you feel weak which prevents you from doing bad things and helps you to overcome Maya (illusion).

One must try to keep fast on the day of Ekadashi. If this cannot be achieved, one should keep falahar, take only fruit. If this cannot be done then one should not consume anaj, being pulses and grains.

These days we eat many rich types of foods on Ekadashi. This defeats the whole purpose and ethos of Ekadashi. On this day we are supposed to lead simple lives and not indulge in eating exotic foods (chips, bhajyas, etc.).

In the medical world, it is widely accepted that fasting for one day and simply taking water is very beneficial for the body. This is also the case when just consuming fruit. It is amazing that the concept of Ekadashi and fasting is an ancient tradition of our religion, whose benefits are only now being realised in society today.

On Ekadashi you should concentrate upon Lord Swaminarayan. We should aim to please God on this day by singing kirtans, chanting dhoon and performing devotion. Satsangis must make special effort to attend temple for darshan of God. This is the one and only way to keep your mind and body healthy.

The Satangijeevan states that not observing Ekadashi is a great sin, and those souls will suffer in the afterlife. Ekadashi happens to be the highest form of self-virtue in that you can achieve maximum goals to satisfy Lord Swaminarayan. You could say that it is a test to see how well you can control your senses.

Diwali and Ankoot

The Diwali festival spans over several days and consists of the festivals of Dhan Teras, Kali Chaudas, Laxmi Poojan, Diwali, Ankoot and Bhai beej.

On Dhan Teras houses are decorated with candles and cows are colourfully decorated. The main decoration in a house is covering the doorstep with Rangoli patterns to welcome guests.

Kalichaudas has been specially nominated for Hanuman and pooja is offered to him on this day. Coconuts and sweetballs, made from sesame seeds are offered to Hanuman at temple and at home.

Diwali originally comes from the Sanskrit word "Deepavali", which means a row of lights. Lord Ram returned to Ayodhya on Diwali after being exiled for a period of fourteen years. He returned to Ayodhya with Sita and Laxman. At the time, people of Ayodhya lit lamps to mark the home coming of Lord Ram.

Laxmi poojan is performed on the day of Diwali. Prayers are offered to the Goddess of Wealth, Laxmiji, so that one may gain prosperity. All throughout the world, Hindus light fireworks to mark the last day of the Vikram Samvat year.

Ankoot falls of the day after Diwali. Ankoot literally means 'grand offering to God'. In our society and religion, grand celebrations take place on this day. Finely prepared, rich food is offered to God and this is then served as prasad. Family and friends greet each other to mark the coming of the New Year, and wish each other well.

On this day Lord Krishna lifted Mount Govardhan to protect the people of Gokul and Vrindavan from the heavy rains caused by Lord Indra. Ankoot is first offered to Mount Govardhan and then to God.

On Bhai-Beej sisters show their love and gratitude for their brothers. The sister invites her brothers to have a special meal at her home. This is to show the sister's appreciation for all the gifts and help she receives from her brothers.

Tulsi Vivaha

Tulsi Vivaha is celebrated on Prabodhini Ekadashi and spans over a total of five days, in the first month of the new VS year. The festival commemorates the wedding between Tulsi and Lord Vishnu. Tulsi Vivaha is celebrated in a grand manner at all Swaminarayan temples.

Vasant Panchmi

This is the auspicious day when Lord Swaminarayan completed compiling the divine Shikshapatri on the 5th day of the bright half of the month of Maha in VS 1882.

Vasant Panchmi also marks the start of the spring season in India.

Chaturmas

"All My followers shall perform additional religious duties during the four months of monsoon and those who are incapable of doing this, shall perform them at least during the month of Shravan."
(Shikshapatri Sloka 76)

The four months of the monsoon season are termed Chaturmas. Chaturmas spans from Devshayani Ekadashi, in the month of Ashadh, through the months of Shravan, Bhadarvo, Aaso and through to Prabodhini Ekadashi in the month of Kartik, the first month of the New Year.

The significance of Chaturmas is for satsangis to observe extra penance. Satsangis observe self-control through their senses and abstain from worldly pleasure to gain affection and love of Lord Swaminarayan.

Dhanurmas

Dhanurmas is a festival that is celebrated during the month of Magsar. In this month Lord Krishna went to Sandeepani Rishi's ashram for education.

Satsangis remember this month for God, by preparing rich foods for Him. The food is prepared and offered in the morning to help God during the days when He attended the ashram of Sandeepani Rishi.

Hindola

Hindola festival is celebrated during the months of Ashadh and Shravan, which fall in the monsoon season.

For an entire month, the murti of Lord is placed in a hindola.

Lord Swaminarayan stands on the twelve face Hindola

The devotees celebrate the festival by performing aarti of Lord residing in the hindola, singing kirtans praising Lord and swaying the hindola of Lord.

The hindola festival originates from the period of Lord Krishna in Vrindavan, over 5000 years ago. In Vrindavan, the women devotees often swayed Lord Krishna when He sat on a hindola, a decorated swing.

Lord Shree Swaminarayan was adored by satsangis. In Vadtal, Nishkulanand Swami constructed a twelve-faced hindola from the frame of two mango trees. The devotees joyfully and with great love swayed the Lord whilst He sat on the hindola. Lord Swaminarayan truly appreciated the love of His devotees and whilst standing in the hindola, appeared in twelve different divine forms and blessed the devotees.

The hindola festival is celebrated with great love and devotion in temples. Devotees spend great time and effort in making beautiful and decorative hindolas for Lord.

Sharad Poonam

Sharad Poonam is the day of the year when the moon is at its brightest. It falls on the last day of the bright half of the month of Aaso.

On Sharad Poonam, Lord Swaminarayan held huge raas festivals in the open air, under the light of the bright moon. One famous instance occurred in Panchala on Sharad

Poonam, as depicted in the kirtan 'Juo juo sahelio aaj Rasio raas raame...' by Acharya Shree Viharilalji Maharaj. Here Lord Swaminarayan played raas with other satsangis, He assumed multiple forms and He simultaneously played raas with all the satsangis. Lord Krishna is famed to have played raas with the gopis on Sharad Poonam along the banks of the Yamuna River.

Holi

Holika was the sister of the demon King Hiranyakashipu. Although the King was a demon he had a son called Prahalada, who was a great devotee of God. Hiranyakashipu considered himself to be Lord of the universe and was forever against his son having such strong belief in God.

The demon nature of King Hiranyakashipu made him take severe action against his own son and tried to kill him.

King Hiranyakashipu persuaded his sister, Holika, to help him in killing Prahalada simply because of his devoted belief in God. Holika agreed to be a part of this demonic act.

Holika had been granted a boon in the form of a fireproof shawl, which would prevent her from being burnt by fire. Holika and Hiranyakashipu planned to kill Prahalada by burning him, whilst she wore her protective shawl. She entered the fire with Prahalada with the intention of killing him. Instead the wind blew the shawl away from Holika and onto Prahalada. Prahalada was saved but Holika was burnt to death as she was misusing her powers in trying to kill a devotee.

Holi is celebrated with the throwing of coloured powder, welcoming the spring season in India on the 15th day of the bright half of the month of Falgun. It symbolises that good always defeats evil.

Rakshabandhan

Rakshabandhan is a popular festival in the Hindu calendar, celebrated in the month of Shravan. On this festival, sisters traditionally tie a saffron coloured thread, a raakhi, around the wrist of the right hand of their brothers and in return the brothers give them gifts. Sisters pray for their brother's protection and the brothers undertake to protect their sisters from any evil influence.

Actually the practise is not only restricted to brothers and sisters but may be extended to men outside the family who accept the obligation to be ready to help women when in need.

In the view of most people, Rakshabandhan has an important message for society, in that it creates a bond to protect and safeguard the well being of sisters, who may in some places be threatened.

Makar Sakranti

Makar literally means 'Capricorn' and Sakranti is when the sun passes from one sign of the zodiac to the next. The Sakranti of any month is considered lucky as it represents a fresh start. On this day satsangis make a concerted effort to perform bhakti and offer gifts to God, in return for blessings on this auspicious day.

Makar Sakranti is celebrated in the month of Maha when the sun enters the zodiac of Makar. This day marks the end of a long winter with the return of the sun to the Northern Hemisphere. This festival is unique in that it always falls on the same date of the Gregorian calendar, 14th January each year.

Jal Jilni

Jal Jilni is celebrated on the 11th day of the bright half of the month of Bhadarvo. On this day Lord Krishna went to bathe in the Yamuna River with many friends with great love and affection.

Rath Yatra

This is the festival where Lord Jagannath (Lord Krishna) is taken on a procession and a parade is performed, where procession floats are pulled by hand and not animals. It is celebrated on the 2nd day of the bright half of the month of Ashadh. On this day Lord Krishna went to visit His masi.

Hindu calendar

The Hindu calendar system is based upon the motion of the moon. Each lunar year comprises twelve months. The lunar year comprises 354 days, compared to 365 ¼ days of the Gregorian calendar, which is based on the solar system.

This gap increases to a month over a period of three years. For this reason, the Hindu lunar calendar has an extra month every three years, named Adhik.

The month of Adhik is considered to be more auspicious, and is referred to as the month of Purushottam, God. Those observing extra penance, bhakti and benevolence during this month gain extra blessings from God and their sins are washed away. During this month auspicious events such as weddings are avoided.

The counting of the years of the Hindu calendar commenced from the birth of King Vikram Samvat. It is for this reason that Hindu dates are prefixed with VS, to define Vikram Samvat.

The Hindu months and the Gregorian calendar months are as follows:

1	Kartik	October – November
2	Magsar	November – December
3	Poash	December – January
4	Maha	January – February
5	Falgun	February – March
6	Chaitra	March – April
7	Vaishakh	April – May
8	Jyeshth	May – June
9	Ashadh	June – July
10	Shravan	July – August
11	Bhadarvo	August – September
12	Aaso	September – October

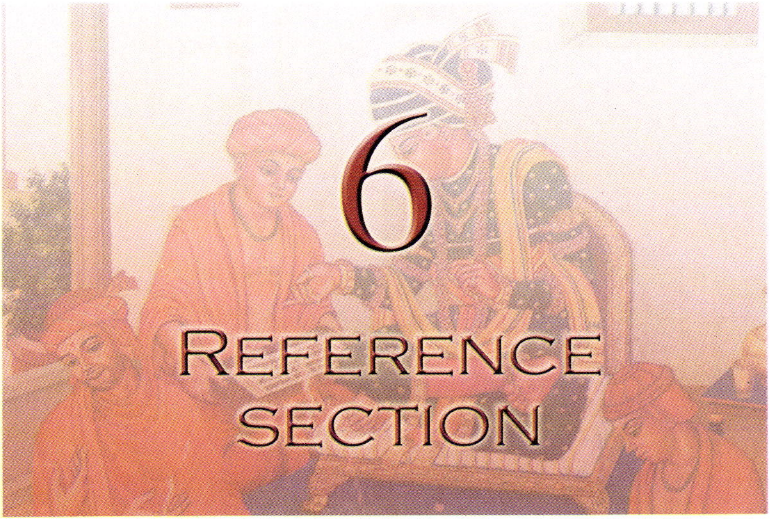

6 Reference section

Image of Lord Swaminarayan's Cheens

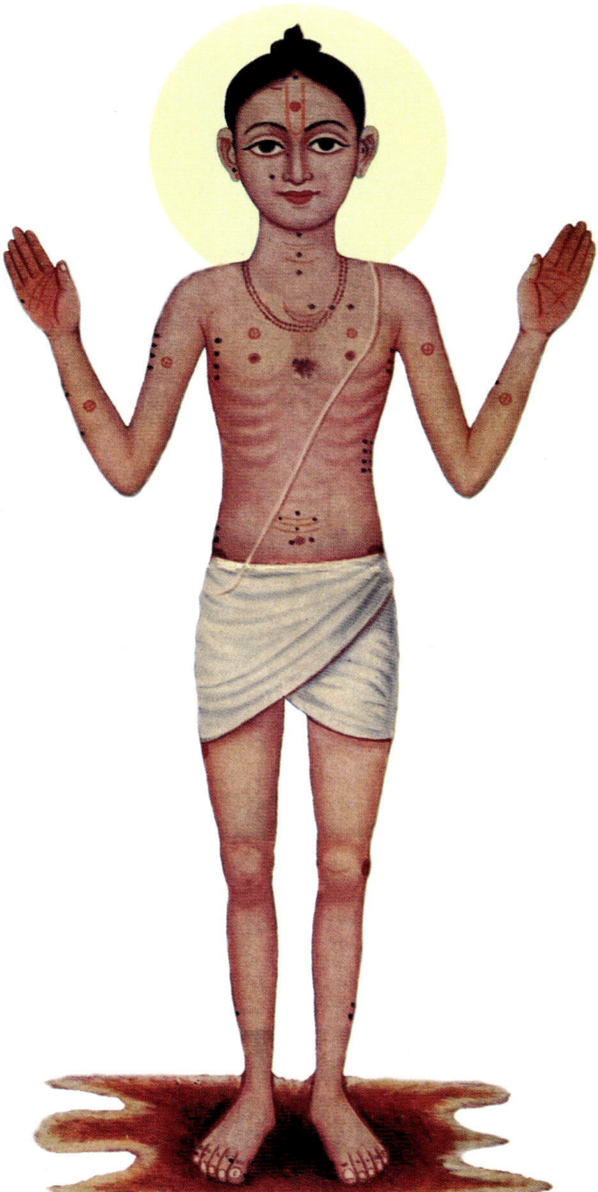

Image of Lord Swaminarayan's Cheens

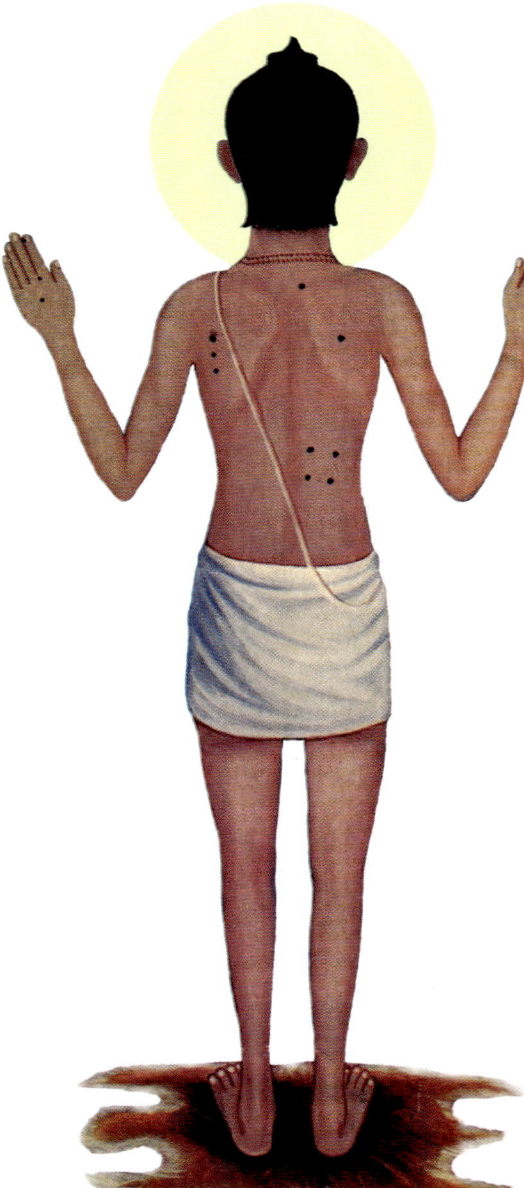

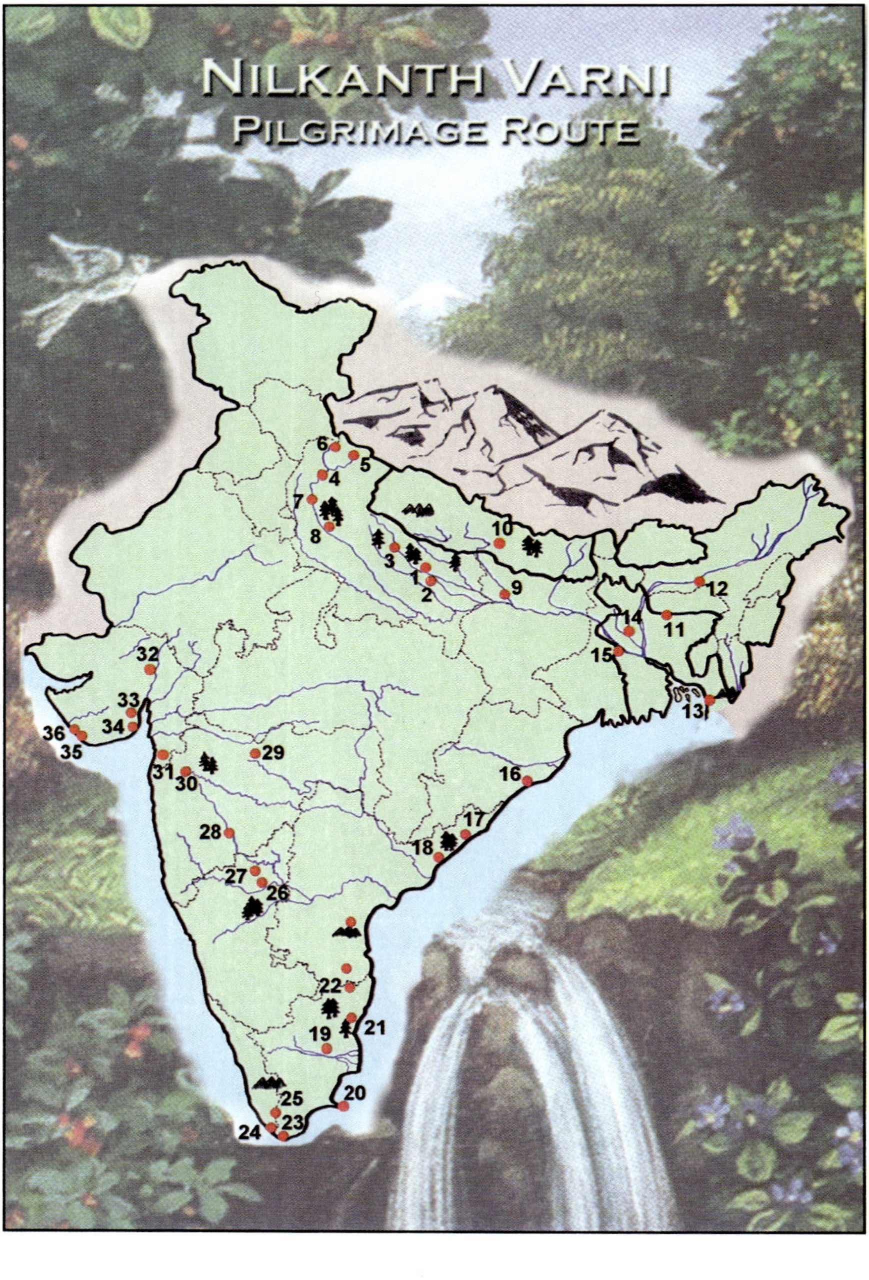
NILKANTH VARNI
PILGRIMAGE ROUTE
1
2
3
4
5
6
7
8
9
10
11
12
13
14
15
16
17
18
19
20
21
22
23
24
25
26
27
28
29
30
31
32
33
34
35
36

NILKANTH VARNI
PILGRIMAGE ROUTE
1. Chhapaiya
2. Ayodhya
3. River Saryu
4. Seerpur
5. Badrinath
6. Kedarnath
7. Haridwar
8. Pulhashram
9. River Gandki
10. Butolnagar
11. Seerpur
12. Chutargam
13. Mount Navlakha
14. Ganga Sagar
15. Kapilashram
16. Jagannathpuri
17. Adi Kurma
18. Manaspur
19. Shri Rangkshetra
20. Rameshwar
21. Large deep forest
22. Bhutpuri
23. Kumarika Khetra
24. Padmanabh
25. Adi Keshav
26. Kishkindha
27. Lake Pampa
28. Pandharpur
29. Burhanpur
30. Nasik
31. Dharampur
32. Jetalpur
33. Bhimnath
34. Gopnath
35. Mongrol
36. Loj

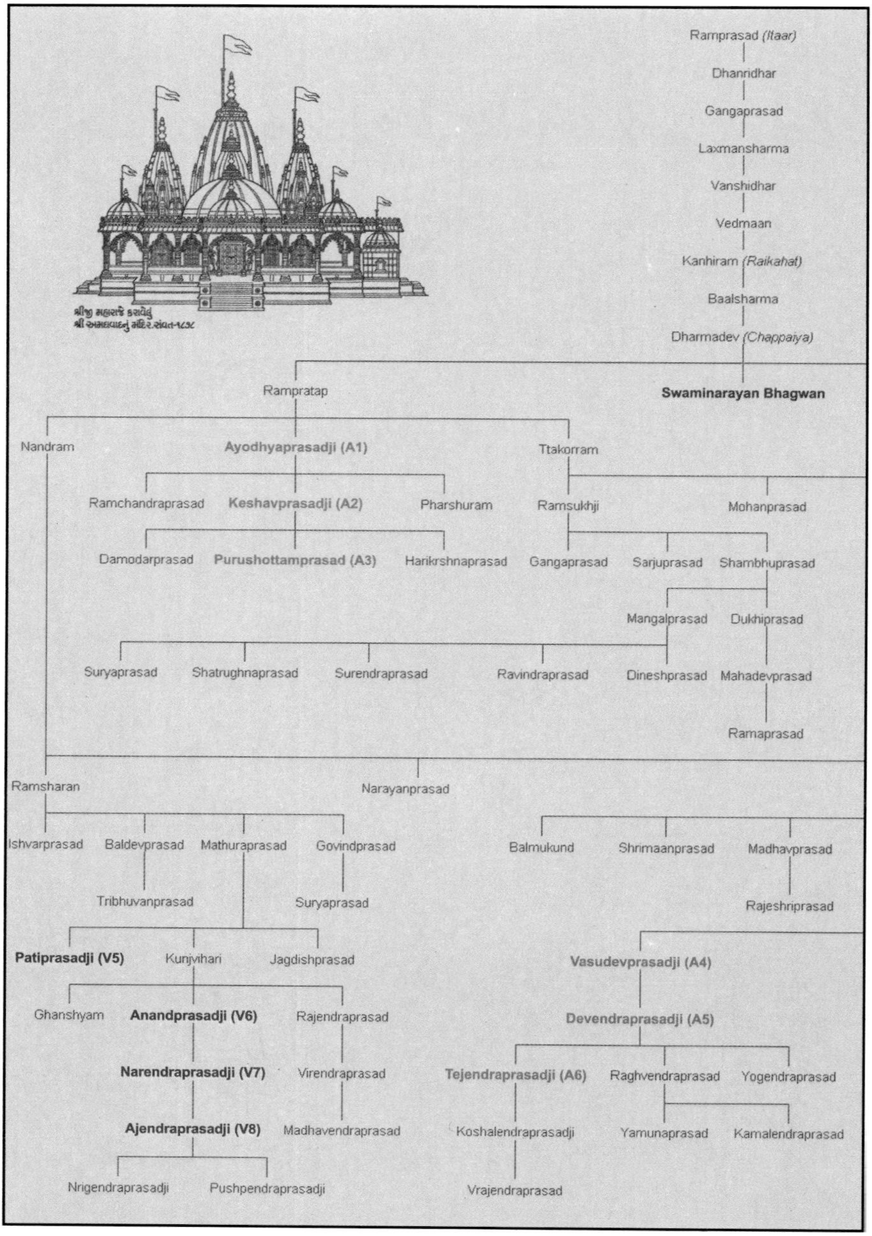
Ramprasad (Itaar)
Dhanridhar
Gangaprasad
Laxmansharma
Vanshidhar
Vedmaan
Kanhiram (Raikahat)
Baalsharma
Dharmadev (Chappaiya)
Rampratap
Swaminarayan Bhagwan
Nandram
Ayodhyaprasadji (A1)
Ttakorram
Ramchandraprasad
Keshavprasadji (A2)
Pharshuram
Ramsukhji
Mohanprasad
Damodarprasad
Purushottamprasad (A3)
Harikrshnaprasad
Gangaprasad
Sarjuprasad
Shambhuprasad
Mangalprasad
Dukhiprasad
Suryaprasad
Shatrughnaprasad
Surendraprasad
Ravindraprasad
Dineshprasad
Mahadevprasad
Ramaprasad
Ramsharan
Narayanprasad
Ishvarprasad
Baldevprasad
Mathuraprasad
Govindprasad
Balmukund
Shrimaanprasad
Madhavprasad
Tribhuvanprasad
Suryaprasad
Rajeshriprasad
Patiprasadji (V5)
Kunjvihari
Jagdishprasad
Vasudevprasadji (A4)
Ghanshyam
Anandprasadji (V6)
Rajendraprasad
Devendraprasadji (A5)
Narendraprasadji (V7)
Virendraprasad
Tejendraprasadji (A6)
Raghvendraprasad
Yogendraprasad
Ajendraprasadji (V8)
Madhavendraprasad
Koshalendraprasadji
Yamunaprasad
Kamalendraprasad
Nrigendraprasadji
Pushpendraprasadji
Vrajendraprasad

DHARMAKUL FAMILY TREE

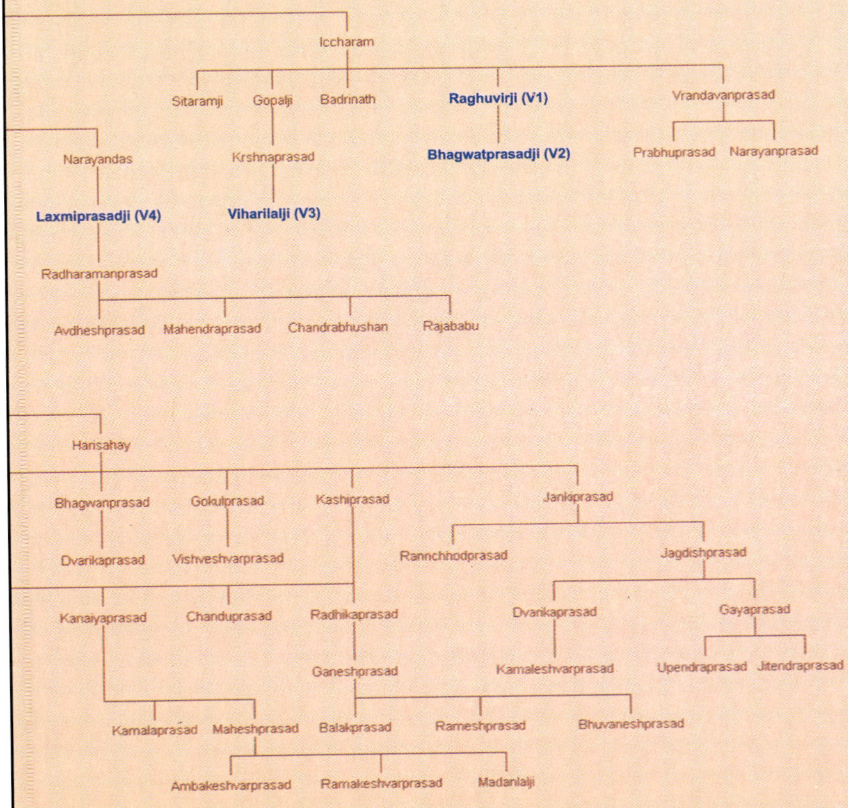

Acharyas:

Ahmedabad Acharyas:

	Name		
1.	Ayodhyaprasad	B: 25 May 1809 D: 18 Feb 1868	I: 10 Nov 1826 A: 42 Years
2.	Keshavprasad	B: 16 Apr 1835 D: 9 Apr 1890	I: 18 Feb 1868 A: 22 Years
3.	Purushottamprasad	B: 7 Feb 1870 D: 25 Nov 1901	I: 9 Apr 1890 A: 12 Years
4.	Vasudevprasad	B: 17 Jul 1899 D: 29 Nov 1937	I: 25 Nov 1901 A: 35 Years
5.	Devendraprasad	B: 5 Oct 1922 D: 12 Oct 1969	I: 30 Nov 1937 A: 32 Years
6.	Tejendraprasad	B: 11 Apr 1944	I: 13 Oct 1969

B – Born
I – Initiation
D – Death
A – Acharya Reign

Vadtal Acharyas:

	Name		
1.	Raghuvir	B: 21 Mar 1812 D: 9 Feb 1863	I: 10 Nov 1826 A: 37 Years
2.	Bhagavatprasad	B: 11 Oct 1838 D: 12 Aug 1879	I: 9 Feb 1863 A: 17 Years
3.	Viharilal	B: 19 Apr 1852 D: 27 Sep 1899	I: 12 Aug 1879 A: 20 Years
4.	Laxmiprasad	B: 15 Aug 1892 D: 24 Apr 1909	I: 27 Sep 1899 A: 10 Years
5.	Shreepatiprasad	B: 18 Aug 1875 D: 12 Feb 1931	I: 26 Apr 1909 A: 22 Years
6.	Anandprasad	B: 22 Jul 1906 D: 8 Jul 1974	I: 12 Feb 1931 A: 28 Years
7.	Narendraprasad	B: 25 Jan 1930	I: 30 Apr 1959
8.	Ajendraprasad	B: 16 Aug 1949	I: 1984

B – Born
I – Initiation
D – Death
A – Acharya Reign

Clothing worn by Lord Swaminarayan

Chronological list of festivals

Festivals	Hindu Months	Gregorian Months
Makar Sakranti	14th January	14thJanuary
Vasant Panchmi, Shikshapatri Jayanti	5th day (B.H.), Maha	January/February
Maha Shivratri	14th day (D.H.), Maha	January/February
NarNarayan Jayanti, Holi	15th day (B.H.), Falgun	February/March
Swaminarayan Jayanti, Ramnavmi	9th day (B.H.), Chaitra	March/April
Rath Yatra	2nd day (B.H.), Ashadh	June/July
Chaturmas	11th day (B.H.), Ashadh	June/July
Hindola	2nd day (D.H.), Ashadh	June/July
Rakshabandhan	Last day (B.H.), Shravan	July/August
Janmashtami	8th day (D.H.), Shravan	July/August
Ganesh Choth	4th day (B.H.), Bhadarvo	August/September
Rushi Panchmi	5th day (B.H.), Bhadarvo	August/September
Jal Jilni	11th day (B.H.), Bhadarvo	August/September
Vaman Jayanti	12th day (B.H.), Bhadarvo	August/September
Sharad Poonam	Last day (B.H.), Aaso	September/October
Dhan Teras	13th day (D.H.), Aaso	October/November
Kali Chaudas	14th day (D.H.), Aaso	October/November
Diwali	Last day (D.H.), Aaso	October/November
Ankoot	1st day (B.H.), Kartik	October/November
Bhai Beej	2nd day (B.H.), Kartik	October/November
Tulsi Vivaha	11th day (B.H.), Kartik	October/November
Dhanurmas	2nd day (B.H.), Magsar	November/December

B.H. = Bright Half

D.H. = Dark Half

Shikshapatri slokas summary

Introductory slokas 1-10

1	Manglacharan - Meditation upon the Lord.
2	Shikshapatri written in Vadtal for all satsangis.
3 - 6	Lord's blessings upon each of the classification groups of Acharyas, Naishtika Brahmcharis, Married and Widowed Women, Saints, Householders and all satsangis. Ideal devotee of each group highlighted.
7	Purpose of writing Shikshapatri to ensure ultimate well being of all mankind.
8	Those who follow the Shikshapatri achieve ultimate bliss.
9	Those who do not abide by the Shikshapatri will suffer great distress.
10	Abide by Shikshapatri willingly and with vigilance.

Dharmas for all Satsangis 11-122

11	Shall not kill any living beings.
12	Shall not sacrifice living beings.
13	Shall not kill for personal gain.
14	Shall not commit suicide.
15	Shall never take meat or alcohol.
16	Shall not harm oneself or others.
17	Shall not commit theft.
18	Shall not commit adultery, gambling or take intoxicants.
19	Should not take food from improper sources.
20	Should not make false accusations against others or verbally abuse.
21	Should not slander.
22	Should not accept prasad where meat or alcohol is offered to the deity.
23	Should be respectful to all deities.
24	Should not give up one's religious duties, nor follow duties prescribed for others or those that are pretentious or fictitious.
25	Should not listen to preachings from improper people.

26 Should withhold the truth if it will endanger life. Should avoid company of ungrateful people and shall not accept bribes.
27 Should not associate with improper and sinful people.
28 Should not associate with hypocrites.
29 Shall not listen to scriptures which deny the existence of God.
30 Shall filter milk and water before consumption nor bathe in water containing organisms.
31 Should not consume medication which contains meat or alcohol or prescribed by unknown physicians.
32 Should not foul or spit in inappropriate places.
33 Should not enter or exit secretly, should not lodge without owner's permission.
34 Male followers should not listen to religious discourse given by females. Never associate with women who have contact with rulers or prominent people.
35 Shall never insult respected people.
36 Should carry out religious actions immediately. Should perform other acts with careful consideration. Should impart knowledge onto others.
37 Should always bear gifts for God, Guru and Rulers. Should not be egotistic or betray someone's trust.
38 Shall not wear inappropriate or revealing clothing.
39 Should not practice devotion without righteousness.
Should not give up devotion due to criticism.
40 Shall segregate male and female assemblies during temple services.
41 Shall wear a twin-thread kanthi made of Tulsi. Should make a tilak mark on the forehead, both arms and on the chest.
42 Should make the tilak mark from Gopichandan.
43 Should make chandlo mark in the middle of tilak from kumkum or Gopichandan.
44 Sat-shudras who follow their dharma should wear twin-thread tulsi kanthis and make tilak marks.

45	Other social groups shall not make tilak marks, but can make chandlo mark. They shall wear kanthi made from any wood except tulsi duly offered to God.
46	Brahmins who now follow Lord Swaminarayan need not give up their heritage of marking the Tripundra or wearing Rudraksha.
47	Shall treat Lord Narayan and Lord Shiva as equal.
48	Shall not use concessions granted in scriptures for extreme hardships in trivial situations.
49 - 54	Should perform daily morning rituals of bathing, prayer etc.
55 - 60	Great devotees (Atmanivedis) should perform these daily rituals by also offering flowers, fruit etc. Should never consume food without offering to God first.
61	Any followers unable to care for their pooja, should give them to others who can but should continue to serve God to the best of their ability.
62	Shall worship those idols that have been blessed by the Acharya.
63	Should go to temple every evening and chant the Lord's name.
64	Should listen to and read scriptures and celebrate festivals with music.
65	Should read all religious scriptures on a regular basis.
66	Shall always assign jobs to those able to carry out the task.
67	Should ensure any staff are fully looked after.
68	Shall treat people with due respect according to their status and situation.
69	Should be courteous and welcoming to all respected people.
70	Should show respect by sitting in a respectable posture.
71	Should not argue with the Acharya. Should offer them gifts.
72	Should always accompany the Acharya when welcoming him and bidding him farewell.

73	Shall not give up Dharma in hope of some other benefits.
74	Should only follow the good deeds of great people.
75	Should not disclose other people's secrets. Should give due respect to people after considering all their merits.
76-78	Should observe additional penance and devotion during Chaturmas.
79	Should observe fast on Ekadashis and birthdays of the Lord.
80	Should avoid sleeping and sexual indulgence during the daytime on days of fast.
81 - 82	Should perform penance, rites and pooja as described by Shri Vitthalnathji.
83	Should go on pilgrimage according to their abilities.
84	Shall perform pooja to the five deities recognised by Lord.
85	Should only chant Narayan Kavach or Hanuman Stotra when possessed by evil spirits.
86 - 87	Should observe the rites of eclipses as prescribed.
88	Should observe sutak for births and deaths.
89 - 90	Should perform duties and qualities as prescribed for the four castes.
91	The upper three castes should observe the rites following conception (Sanskars) and rememberance (Shraadh).
92	Shall perform penance for all sins committed.
93 - 95	The eight Hindu scriptures approved by Lord Swaminarayan.
96	All should listen to and Brahmins study, teach and preach the eight scriptures.
97 - 99	The Mitakshara Tika, a commentary upon Yagnavalkya Smruti (Dharma Shastra) should be considered as a guiding authority on daily rites, business affairs and code of expiation. Shreemad Bhagwat's Chapters 5 (Yoga Shastra) and 10 (Bhakti Shastra) describes the greatness and glory of Lord.

100	Ramanuja Acharya's commentaries on Vyaas Sutra and Shreemad Bhagwad Gita- are true underlying philosophies of the Sampraday.
101 -102	The parts of the scriptures referencing the divinity of God, Bhakti, Dharma and Vairagya should be held in high regard.
103	Dharma is the right conduct authenticated by scriptures Bhakti is the profound love for God coupled with the knowledge of the greatness of God.
104	Vairagya is non-attachment to everything except God Gnaan is knowledge of Jeeva, Maya and Ishwar.
105	Jeeva is the indweller of the heart. It is conscious, knowledgeable and pervades the whole body. It is impenetrable, invisible, indivisible, indestructible and eternal.
106	Maya is of the three Gunas. Full of darkness, it creates ego and attachment.
107	Ishwar dwells in the Jeeva. He is supreme and gives rewards according to their acts.
108	Ishwar is Par-Brahm Purushottam, the source of all incarnations.
109 - 111	Various names of the Lord when accompanied by different bhaktas.
112	Should not discriminate between the various multi handed forms of Lord.
113	Shall achieve ultimate salvation only by devotion to Lord.
114	Knowledge alone without Bhakti and Satsang does not attain salvation.
115	Only meditation of Almighty Lord Supreme and His incarnations should be practiced.
116	Should only meditate on the Lord as Brahm by separating oneself from the three forms of body (sthool, sukshma and karan).
117	Should read and listen regularly to Chapter 10 of Shreemad Bhagwat.
118	Should hold katha according to one's means in order to gain desired fruits of life.

119 Should follow conduct that saves oneself and others in times of great difficulty.

120 Should take full consideration of circumstances when carrying out any act.

121 Philosophy is Vishistadwaita, Golok is the Divine Abode. Mukti is the ability to serve God in his greatest form in Golok.

122 The above rules should be observed by everyone.

Dharmas of Acharyas and their Wives 123-134

123 Shall initiate and preach to males only, except blood relations.

124 Shall not touch or speak with females outside the immediate family. Should not be cruel and should not accept things for safe keeping.

125 Shall not stand as guarantee for any person. Shall not incur debts.

126 Should not sell food grains given by followers.

127 Shall perform pooja of Ganpati and Hanuman on specified days.

128 Shall initiate male followers desirous of salvation.

129 Should ensure satsangis follow the righteous path, respect saints and study scriptures.

130 Shall worship idols of Lord in approved temples.

131 Should be hospitable to those who come to temple by offering prasad.

132 Should establish institutions to impart knowledge of scriptures.

133 The wives of the Acharyas (Gadiwala) to initiate females only.

134 Gadiwala not to show her face, touch or talk to any males outside of the immediate family.

Dharmas of Householders 135-156

135 Males shall not touch widows outside of the immediate family.

136 Males shall not reside alone with their mother, sister or daughter who are young except in emergencies. Shall not give away their wife.

137	Males shall not have friendship with women who have contact with prominent people such as rulers.
138	Should be hospitable to guests. Should perform pooja and due rites in memory of ancestors.
139	Shall give lifelong service to parents, guru and the sick.
140	Shall engage in an appropriate occupation according to ones caste and class.
141	Shall save food and money according to the needs of the household.
142	Should only keep animals if you can fully take care of them.
143	Shall always have written records when dealing with property and money.
144	Shall always have witnessed record of any gifts offered in marriage.
145	Should spend within your means.
146	Should always keep regular accounts for income and expenditure.
147	Should give a tenth or twentieth of total income to the Lord annually.
148	Concluding ceremonies of penance (such as Ekadashi) shall be performed according to scriptures in order to gain desired fruits.
149	Should offer worship to Lord Shiva during month of Shravan.
150	Should not borrow anything from temples or Acharyas.
151	Shall not eat food given free of charge either on the way to or at temples and also when visiting saints and gurus.
152	Shall always pay employees as promised Should not conceal clearing of debts or family tree or the daughters engagement. Shall not deal with wicked people.
153 - 154	Shall relocate to somewhere peaceful if under threat of loss of dignity, property or life.
155	Wealthy people should perform non-violent Yagnas and feed brahmins and saints on pilgrimage and auspicious days.

156 Wealthy people should hold large festivals and offer gifts to deserving Brahmins.

Dharmas of Rulers 157-158

157 Shall protect and treat their subjects as if they were their own children. Shall establish a rule of Dharma.

158 Shall acquire all aspects of knowledge of how to rule righteously.

Dharmas of Married Women 159-162

159 Shall serve and respect their husbands.

160 Shall not socialise with other men.

161 Must not wear revealing clothes. Should not watch shows containing abusive or disgraceful behaviour. Should not make acquaintances with immoral women.

162 Should not enjoy merriment when their husbands are away.

Dharmas of Widows 163-172

163 Should serve the Lord as she would have her husband. Should not take decisions without consent from the family.

164 Should not touch or talk to youthful males outside of the immediate family.

165 May touch infants or talk to elderly men when absolutely necessary.

166 Shall not be taught by males outside of the immediate family. Shall regularly observe penance by fasting.

167 Shall only make donations if they have the means to do so.

168 Should eat once a day, sleep on a hard surface and avoid looking at animals mating.

169 Should dress simply and appropriately.

170 Shall not associate with women who have carried out an abortion or indulge in amorous talk about men.

171	Young widows shall not reside with young male friends or relatives.
172	Shall not take part in Holi celebrations. Shall not adorn jewellery or wear glittery clothes.

Dharmas of all Females 173-174

173	Shall always bathe clothed. Shall not conceal their period of menstruation.
174	Shall follow rules of menstruation as prescribed. All the rules for householders should be observed by the Acharyas and their wives.

Dharmas of Naishthika Brahmcharis 175-187

175	Shall not touch, speak to or look at females.
176	Shall not listen to or talk about females. Should not bathe at places frequented by females.
177	Shall never touch or look at pictures or statues of females except those of a deity.
178	Shall not make images of a female. Shall not touch clothing worn by a female. Shall avoid looking at animals mating.
179	Should not acquaint with males who dress like women. Shall not hold religious discourses aimed at women.
180	Should not break their vow of celibacy even if instructed by their guru. Shall remain contented, patient and humble.
181	Should stop women from deliberately approaching them.
182	Should talk to or touch females to save either of their lives.
183	Shall not massage their body with oils. Shall not carry weapons or wear frightful clothing. Shall suppress their sense of taste.
184	Shall only go for food where it is served by males.
185	Shall study the scriptures and serve their guru. Shall not associate with effeminate males.
186	Should not drink from leather vessels. Shall not consume onion, garlic and the like.

187 Shall perform all necessary rites before eating.

Dharmas of Sadhus 188-196

188 Shall not touch, speak to or look at females. Shall not associate with effeminate males. Must defeat inner enemies of lust, anger, greed, pride, etc.

189 Shall control all senses, especially taste. Shall not accumulate wealth personally or by others.

190 Shall not take safe custody of others possessions. Shall always control their temper. Shall never allow women to enter their place of residence.

191 Should not go out alone except in emergencies.

192 Should not wear high quality or colourful clothing.

193 Should not visit any individual's home except for religious reasons. Shall use all spare time for devotion to God.

194 - 195 Shall only go for food where it is prepared and served by males. Shall otherwise cook from raw provisions for themselves.

196 Shall behave in a manner like Bharatji, son of Rushabhdev.

Dharmas common to Naishthika Brahmcharis and Sadhus 197-202

197 Shall abstain from taking intoxicants.

198 Shall not consume food or offerings prepared for rites pertaining to Sanskars or Shraadh.

199 Should not sleep during the day unless ill. Should not get involved in idle gossip.

200 Should not sleep on a bed unless ill. Shall be respectful in front of other sadhus.

201 Should not retaliate if beaten or abused by wicked people.

202 Should not spy for others or slander others. Shall resist all feelings of pride and remove any attachment towards relatives.

Concluding slokas 203 - 212

203 All satsangis should refer to the Sampraday Shastras for further details on all the above slokas.

204 This Shikshapatri is the extracted essence from all the Shastras. It will bring the desired fruits of life.

205 Always behave as prescribed in the Shikshapatri.

206 The four desired objects of life are only achieved by following the Shikshapatri.

207 Those who do not follow the Shikshapatri are deemed not to be part of the Sampraday.

208 - 209 This Shikshapatri should be read, listened to or worshipped daily.

210 The Shikshapatri should only be given to people with good virtues.

211 The Shikshapatri was written by the Lord on Vasant Panchmi (VS 1882) (1826AD) and is the route to ultimate salvation.

212 May the Lord shower blessings on all His followers.

Principle of Ekadashi (Gujarati)

એકાદશી માહાત્મ્ય

એકાદશીના વ્રતનો મહિમા અધિક છે, કારણ કે એકાદશી ભગવાનના શરીરમાંથી ઉત્પન થયેલી છે. એકાદશી ઉત્પન થવાનું કારણ પૂર્વે સત્ય યુગમાં નાડીજંઘનો દીકરો મુરદાનવ મહાન અસુર હતો. બ્રહ્માની આરાધના કરીને અવધ્ય બની ગયો. ત્યાર બાદ કોઈથી તેનું મૃત્યુ ન થાય તેવો વર બ્રહ્મા પાસેથી માંગ્યો હતો. ઊધત બની ગયેલા મુરદાનવે સ્વર્ગ જીતી લીધું. પછી બ્રહ્મા, શિવજી, તથા દેવતાઓ ભગવાનની આરાધના કરવા લાગ્યા. ત્યારે વૈકુંઠપતિ ભગવાન નારાયણે દર્શન દીધાં. ત્યારે દેવોએ પોતાના દુઃખનું નિવેદન કર્યું . ત્યારે ભગવાન અને દેવો મુરદાનવની સાથે યુધ્ધે ચડયા. ત્યારે મુરદાનવનો માર ખાઇને દેવો નાસવા લાગ્યા.

એક હજાર વર્ષ સુધી યુધ્ધ ચાલ્યું. ભગવાન સુદર્શન ચક્રથી પણ મુરદાનવને મારી ન શકયા, છેવટે સિંહવતી ગુફામાં જઈને દશ ઇન્દ્રિયો અને અગિયારમું મન અંતર સન્મુખ કરીને પોઢયા હતા. પાછળ પડેલો મુરદાનવ સિંહવતી ગુફામાં આવ્યો. તે વખતે ભગવાનને મુરદાનવ ઉપર ક્રોધ થયો, એટલે અગિયારે ઇન્દ્રિયોના તેજમાંથી દિવ્ય આયુધવાળી, તપસ્વીની એક કન્યા ઉત્પન થઇ. એ કન્યાને જોતાં જ મોહ પામી ગયેલો મુરદાનવ તેને કહેવા લાગ્યો, "તું મારો સ્વીકાર કર." ત્યારે દેવીએ કહ્યું, "મારી એવી પ્રતિજ્ઞા છે, કે યુધ્ધમાં જે મને જીતે તે મારો પતિ થાય." તે સાંભળી મુરદાનવ યુધ્ધે ઉતર્યો, ત્યારે દેવીએ તલવાર વડે મુરદાનવનું માથું કાપી નાખ્યું.

તેથી સર્વ દેવો તથા ભગવાન રાજી થઇ ગયા અને રાજી થઇને પૂછયું. "તમે કોનાં પુત્રી છો?" દેવી કહે છે. "હે ભગવાન તમારી એકાદશ ઇન્દ્રિયોના તેજમાંથી મારી ઉત્પતિ થઇ છે એટલે મારું નામ એકાદશી છે. હું તમારી શકિત છું, તપરૂપી તેજમાંથી ઉત્પન થઇ એટલે તપત્સ્વીની છું." ભગવાને રાજી થઇ વર માગવાનું કહ્યું. એટલે એકાદશી કહે છે, "હે પ્રભુ, મારા ઉપર રાજી થયા છો તો મને એ વર આપો કે મારું વ્રત કરનાર સર્વે અતિ સુખી થાય અને એના શુભ મનોરથો પૂર્ણ થાય, તેમજ તેના સર્વ પાપ બળી જાય. હે ભગવાન સ્વર્ગ, મૃત્યુ, પાતાળ, સત્ય, ત્રેતા, દ્વાપર અને કળિ યુગમાં અને બાર માસમાં મારું વ્રત ચાલુ રહે, એ વરદાન આપો. તથા હે ભગવાન, બાર મહિનામાં મારા ચોવીસ વ્રત આવે છે, તો તમે ચોવીસ અવતાર ધારણ કરીને મારા પતિ થાવ.

એકાદશીના દિવસે સવારમાં લક્ષ્મીએ સહિત શ્રી કૃષ્ણનું આદર પૂર્વક પૂજન કરવું. અને શકિત અનુસાર થાળ જમાડવા. અને સાંજે સર્વ એકાદશીઓના પતિ રાધાના સ્વામી દામોદર ભગવાનનું પૂજન કરવું. પહેલી એકાદશી માગસર સુદ મોક્ષદા નામની એકાદશી માનેલી છે. આ એકાદશીના દિવસે શ્રી લક્ષ્મીજી નામનાં પત્નીએ સહિત શ્રી કેશવ નામે ભગવાનની માલતી પુષ્પોથી પુજા કરવી.

એકાદશી વ્રત દાન નિયમ

તિથિ	એકાદશી	કૃષ્ણ ભગવાનના નામો	લક્ષ્મીજીના નામો	નૈવેધ્યમાં થાળ
મગશર સુદ	મોક્ષદા	શ્રી કેશવ	શ્રી	લાડુ
માગશર વદ	સફલા	સંકર્ષણ	સુનંદા	લકડશી લાડુ
પોષ સુદ	નંદા (પુત્રદા)	નારાયણ	પદ્મા	ચુરમુ
પોષ વદ	તિલદા (ષટ્તિલા)	વસુદેવ	શ્રીપ્રિયા	ઘેબર
મહા સુદ	જયા	માધવ	નિત્યા	માંડા
મહા વદ	વિજયા	પ્રધ્યુમ્ન	ઘી	સુંવાળીયો (સેવ)
ફાગણ સુદ	છાત્રી આમલકી	ગોવિંદ	ચંદ્રવતી	કંસાર
ફાગણ વદ	પાપમોચની	અનિરૂદ્ધ	સુશીલા	ઘઉંની સેવ
ચૈત્ર સુદ	કામદા	વિષ્ણુ	રમા	દાળના લાડુ
ચૈત્ર વદ	વરૂથિની	પુરૂષોત્તમ	નંદા	વડાં
વૈશાખ સુદ	મોહિની	મધુસૂદન	માધવી	દૂધપાક
વૈશાખ વદ	અપરા	અધોક્ષજ	ત્રયી	દૂધ અને ભાત
જેઠ સુદ	નિર્જલા	ત્રિવિક્રમ	પદમાક્ષી	દહીં અને ભાત
જેઠ વદ	યોગિની	નૃસિંહ	ક્ષેમંકરી	પેંડા
અષાઢ સુદ	દેવશયની	વમન	કમલા	પુરીઓ
અષાઢ વદ	કામિકા	અચયુત	વિજ્યા	ખાજા
શ્રાવણ સુદ	પુત્રદા	શ્રીધર	કાંતિમતી	માલપૂવા
શ્રાવણ વદ	અજા	જનાર્દન	સુંદરી	ગોળના લાડુ
ભાદરવો સુદ	પદ્મા (પરિવર્તિની)	ઋષિકેશ	અપરાજીત	તલ સાંકળી
ભાદરવો વદ	ઇન્દિરા	ઉપેન્દ્ર	સુભગાદેવી	જલેબી
આસો સુદ	પાશાંકુશા	પદ્મનાભ	પદ્મવતી	હરિસો
આસો વદ	રમા	હરિ	હિરણ્યા	કેળાં
કાર્તિક સુદ	પ્રબોધિની	ડામોદર	રાધા	મગદળ
કાર્તિક વદ	અભયા (ઉત્પતિ)	કૃષ્ણા	સુલક્ષણા	બીરંજ
અધિક માસ	કમલા	પુરૂષોત્તમ		

સર્વ એકાદશીઓની વસ્તુઓના અભાવના ફળમાં સોપારી આપવી. પુષ્પોના અભાવમાં તુલસી પત્ર આપવાં, નૈવેધ્યના અભાવમાં સાકરની કણી આપવી. તેમજ દાનના અભાવમાં પોતપોતાની શકિત પ્રમાણેજ તાંદુલ આદી અન્ન આપવું. આ બધુ પ્રયત્ન કરવા છતાં ન મળે તો જ એમ કરવું.

તિથિ	પુષ્પનાં નામો	(અર્ધ્ય) ફળની પૂજા	દાન માટે વાનગીઓ
માગશર સુદ	માલતી	નારંગી	ડાંગર, કંગ, તલ, ઘઉ, જ્વ, સામો, મગ
માગશર વદ	અગસ્તિ	જામફળ	સોનાનું દાન
પોષ સુદ	કુંભી	દાડમ	ઘીનું ભરેલું પાત્ર
પોષ વદ	કલ્હાર (સ્થળ કમળો)	દ્રાક્ષ	વસ્ત્રનું દાન
મહા સુદ	બકુલ (બોરસડી પુષ્પ)	બીજરૂ	આઠ શેર તલથી ભરેલુ તાંબાનું પાત્ર (૩.૫ કિલ્લો)
મહા વદ	તુલસી પત્ર	લીબું	પગરખાં
ફાગણ સુદ	મંદાર (ગુલદા વદી)	અખરોટ	તલ ભરેલું તાંબાનું પાત્ર
ફાગણ વદ	મોગરાનાં (કુદં)	કાકડી ફળ	તલ અથવા ગાય
ચૈત્ર સુદ	આંબા મોર	ચિભડાનું ફળ	ઘીથી પકાવેલ વાનગી
ચૈત્ર વદ	ચંપા	જાયફળ	પૃથ્વીનું દાન
વૈશાખ સુદ	મોગરાનાં પુષ્પો	ફણસ ફળ	શય્યાદાન
વૈશાખ વદ	કેતક	બોફલી	વત્સ સહિત ગાયનું દાન
જેઠ સુદ	જુઇ	આંબાફળ (કેરી)	છત્ર
જેઠ વદ	ભંગરાજ	જાંબુ	જલ ગાયનું દાન
અષાઢ સુદ	અંગેડી	નાળિયેર (શ્રીફળ)	સુવર્ણની ગાય
અષાઢ વદ	પારિજાત	બીલીનાં ફળ	સ્ત્રી પુરૂષોએ ધારણ કરવા યોગ્ય વસ્ત્રો
શ્રાવણ સુદ	શત પત્રકમળ	સીતાફળ	પાદુકા (ચંપલ)
શ્રાવણ વદ	શેણ	સોપારી	ભેંસ
ભાદરવો સુદ	કાશ	કોળા	બાપુરી
ભાદરવો વદ	દૂર્વાકુંરો	આંબળીફળ	કન્યાદાન
આસો સુદ	શમડી	મદન	લાડુ
આસો વદ	સતિ પડાનાં	કેળાં	ઘી સાકર
કાર્તિક સુદ	કમાળો (કમળ)	પદ્મફળ	પલંગ
કાર્તિક વદ	તિલ (તલ)		બલીર્વદ
અધિક માસ			

Swaminarayan Sampraday Scriptures (Gujarati)

સ્વામિનારાયણ સંપ્રદાયનાં શાસ્ત્રો

મહારાજના સમકાલિન શાસ્ત્રો

૧ શિક્ષાપત્રી
૨ શ્રીમદ્ સત્સંગિજીવન
૩ વચનામૃત
૪ ભક્તચિંતામણી
૫ હરિદિગ્વિજય

સંપ્રદાયનાં શાસ્ત્રો

૧ શ્રીમદ્ સત્સંગિ ભૂષણ
૨ શ્રી ઘનશ્યામ લીલામૃતસાગર
૩ નિષ્કુળાનંદ કાવ્ય
૪ હરિલીલામૃત
૫ મુક્તાનંદ કાવ્ય

મહારાજનાં માન્ય કરેલાં શાસ્ત્રો

૧ વેદ
૨ વ્યાસસૂત્ર
૩ શ્રીમદ્ ભાગવત
૪ શ્રી વિષ્ણું સહસ્ત્રનામ
૫ શ્રીમદ્ ભગવદ્ગીતા
૬ શ્રી વિદુરનીતિ
૭ શ્રી વાસુદેવ માહાત્મ્ય
૮ યાજ્ઞવલ્કયસ્મૃતિ

મહારાજનાં અધ્યાત્મ શાસ્ત્રો

૧ શ્રીમદ્ ભગવદ્ગીતાનું ભાષ્ય
૨ શ્રીરામાનુજાચાર્યકૃત વ્યાસૂત્રનું શ્રી ભાષ્ય
અધ્યાત્મ = આત્મજ્ઞાન સંબંધી

Meaning of Prayer (Gujarati)

નિત્ય સ્તુતિ - પ્રાર્થના (નિર્વિકલ્પ ઉત્તમ અતિ નિશ્ચે તવ ઘનશ્યામ...)

સ.ગુ.પ્રેમાનંદ સ્વામીએ માગેલી સાત વસ્તુ નીચે મુજબ છે.

૧ **નિશ્ચય**-ભગવાન તમારો નિર્વિકલ્પ નિશ્ચય.

૨ **ભક્તિ**-માહાત્મ્યજ્ઞાને સહિત તમારી એકાન્તિક ભક્તિ.

૩ **દોષ** (અવગુણ)-તમારો સંત થયા બાદ તમારા ભક્તપણામાં દૂષણરૂપ કામક્રોધાદીક દોષો ન રહે.

૪ **દ્રોહ** (ટીકા)-મારાથી તમો અને તમારા ભક્તનો ક્યારેય દ્રોહ ન થાય.

૫ **સમાગમ**-તમારો અને તમારા એકાન્તિક ભક્ત, સંતનો મને સમાગમ આપજો.

૬ **દર્શન** -દાસાનું દાસ એવો હું મને તમારા દર્શન આપજો.

૭ **પાસ** (નજીક)-મને તમારી સમીપે નિવાસ આપજો.

નીચેનાં અગિયાર નિયમો પ્રમાણે વર્તશે તો ઉપરની સાત વસ્તુઓને પામશે.

૧ હિંસા ન કરવી.

૨ પરસ્ત્રીનો સંગ ન કરવો.

૩ માંસ ન ખાવું

૪ મધ (દારૂ) ન પીવો.

૫ વિધવા સ્ત્રીનો સ્પર્શ ન કરવો.

૬ આત્મઘાત ન કરવો.

૭ ચોરી ન કરવી.

૮ કોઈ ઉપર ખોટું કલંક ન આરોપવું.

૯ કોઈ પણ દેવની નિંદા ન કરવી.

૧૦ જેનું ન સ્વીકારી શકાય તેવાના હાથનું રાંધેલ અન્ન ન ખાવું.

૧૧ વિમુખોના મુખથી ભગવાનની કથા-વાર્તા ન સાંભળવી.

Tatvas (Gujarati)

દેહના ચોવીસ તત્વો અને તેના દેવતા

ચોવીસ તત્વનો દેહ

પંચભૂત, પંચપ્રાણ, દશ ઇન્દ્રિયો, ચાર અંતઃકરણ

પંચભૂત

પૃથ્વી	જળ	તેજ	વાયુ	આકાશ
હાડકાં	લોહી	આળસ	સંકોચ	કાયાકાશ
માંસ	વીર્ય	કાન્તિ	ચલન	ઉદરાકાશ
નાડી	મૂત્ર	ભૂખ	ઉત્ક્રમણ	હ્ધ્યાકાશ
ત્વચા	પરસેવો	તરસ	ધાવન	કંઠાકાશ
રોમ	લાળ	નિંદ્રા	પ્રસારણ	શિરાકાશ

પંચપ્રાણ

પ્રાણ	અપાન	સમાન	વ્યાન	ઉદાન

દશ ઇન્દ્રિયો (પંચજ્ઞાન ઇન્દ્રિયો, પંચકર્મ ઇન્દ્રિયો)

પંચજ્ઞાન ઇન્દ્રિયો	શ્રોત્ર	ત્વક્	ચક્ષુ	રસના	ઘ્રાણ
વિષય	શબ્દ	સ્પર્શ	રૂપ	રસ	ગંધ
દેવતા	દિગ્પાળ	વાયુ	સૂર્ય	વરુણ	અશ્વિની કુમાર

પંચકર્મ ઇન્દ્રિયો	વાંક્(વાણી)	પાણી (હાથ)	પાદ (પગ)	પાયુ (મળદ્વાર)	ઉપસ્થ (મૂત્ર દ્વાર)
વિષય	બોલવુ	લેવુ-દેવુ	હાલ-ચાલ	મળત્યાગ	રતિવિલાસ
દેવતા	અગ્નિ	ઇન્દ્ર	ઉપેન્દ્ર	યમરાજ	પ્રજાપતિ

ચાર અંતઃકરણ	મન	બુધ્ધિ	ચિત્	અહંકાર
વિષય	સંકલ્પ-વિકલ્પ	નિશ્ચય	ચિંતવન	અભિમાન
દેવતા	ચંદ્ર	બ્રા	નારાયણ	રુદ્ર

Janmangal (Gujarati)

જનમંગલનામાવલી

૧ **ૐ શ્રીકૃષ્ણાય નમઃ** શ્યામ વર્ણવાળા અને ભકતોના મનને આકર્ષણ કરવાવાળા અને ભકતોના દુઃખને નિર્મૂળ કરનારા રાધા લક્ષ્મીથી યુકત શ્રીહરિને હું નમસ્કાર કરું છું.

૨ **ૐ શ્રી વાસુદેવાય નમઃ** વસુદેવના પુત્ર અને શુધ્ધ અંતઃકરણમાં પ્રગટ થનારા એવા શ્રીહરિને હું નમસ્કાર કરું છું.

૩ **ૐ શ્રી નરનારાયણાય નમઃ** નરની સાથે મનુષ્યોના પ્રવર્તક અથવા સર્વે મનુષ્યોના આશ્રય એવા નારાયણરૂપ શ્રીહરિને હું વંદન કરું છું.

૪ **ૐ શ્રી પ્રભવે નમઃ** અતિ સમર્થ એવા શ્રીહરિને નમસ્કાર કરું છું.

૫ **ૐ શ્રી ભકિતધર્માત્મજાય નમઃ** ભકિતમાતા અને ધર્મદેવ થકી પુત્રરૂપે પ્રગટ થયેલા એવા શ્રીહરિને હું નમસ્કાર કરું છું.

૬ **ૐ શ્રી અજન્મને નમઃ** કર્માધિન જન્મથી રહિત એવા શ્રીહરિને હું વંદન કરું છું.

૭ **ૐ શ્રી કૃષ્ણાય નમઃ** નવીન મેઘ સમાન શ્યામ વર્ણવાળા, અને ભકતોના મનને આકર્ષણ કરનારા, અને ભકતોના દુઃખને નિર્મૂળ કરનારા, એવા શ્રીહરિને હું નમસ્કાર કરું છું.

૮ **ૐ શ્રી નારાયણાય નમઃ** સર્વે જનોના આશ્રયરૂપ અથવા સર્વે જનોના પ્રવર્તક એવા નારાયણ જે શ્રીહરિને હું વંદન કરું છું.

૯ **ૐ શ્રી હરયે નમઃ** ભકતોના દુઃખને હરણ કરનારા એવા શ્રીહરિને હું નમસ્કાર કરું છું.

૧૦ **ૐ શ્રી હરિકૃષ્ણાય નમઃ** ભકતોના દુઃખને હરણ કરનારા અને ભકતોના મનને આકર્ષણ કરનારા એવા શ્રીહરિને હું નમસ્કાર કરું છું.

૧૧ **ૐ શ્રી ઘનશ્યામાય નમઃ** મેઘની સમાન શ્યામ વર્ણવાળા એવા પરમાત્માને હું નમસ્કાર કરું છું.

૧૨ **ૐ શ્રી ધાર્મિકાય નમઃ** સંપૂર્ણ ધર્મોનું પાલન કરનારા એવા શ્રીહરિને હું નમસ્કાર કરું છું.

૧૩ **ૐ શ્રી ભકિતનન્દનાય નમઃ** ભકિતપુત્ર અથવા ભકિતમાતા થકી પ્રગટ થયેલા એવા શ્રીહરિને હું નમસ્કાર કરું છું.

૧૪ **ૐ શ્રી બૃહદ્વ્રતધરાય નમઃ** મહાન બ્રહ્મચર્યવ્રતને ધારણ કરનારા એવા શ્રીહરિને હું વંદન કરું છું.

૧૫ **ૐ શ્રી શુદ્ધાય નમઃ** માયાના ગુણોથી રહિત એવા શુદ્ધ સ્વરૂપ પરમાત્માને હું નમસ્કાર કરું છું.

૧૬ **ૐ શ્રી રાધાકૃષ્ણેષ્ટદૈવતાય નમઃ** રાધાકૃષ્ણદેવને ઈષ્ટદેવપણે સ્વીકારનારા એવા શ્રીહરિને હું નમસ્કાર કરું છું.

૧૭ **ૐ શ્રી મરૂત્સુતપ્રિયાય નમઃ** વાયુપુત્ર હનુમાનજી જેને અતિશય પ્રિય છે એવા શ્રીહરિને હું વંદન કરું છું.

૧૮ **ૐ શ્રી કાલીભૈરવાધ્યતિભીષણાય નમઃ** કાલી ભૈરવ એ આદિ અનેક અસુરોને તથા રાક્ષસોને ભય પમાડનારા એવા શ્રીહરિને હું નમસ્કાર કરું છું.

૧૯ **ૐ શ્રી જિતેન્દ્રિયાય નમઃ** જેમણે પોતાની સર્વે ઈન્દ્રિયોને જીતેલી છે એવા પરમાત્મા શ્રીહરિને હું નમસ્કાર કરું છું.

૨૦ **ૐ શ્રી જિતાહારાય નમઃ** જેમણે પોતાનો આહાર જીતેલો છે અર્થાત નિયમમાં કરેલો છે એવા શ્રીહરિને હું વંદન કરું છું.

૨૧ **ૐ શ્રી તીવ્રવૈરાગ્યાય નમઃ** અતિશય તિવ્ર વૈરાગ્યથી યુકત એવા શ્રીહરિને હું નમસ્કાર કરું છું.

૨૨ **ૐ શ્રી આસ્તિકાય નમઃ** આ લોક તથા પરલોકને સત્ય માનનારા તથા સ્વર્ગ નરકને સ્વીકારનારા એવા પરમાત્મા શ્રીહરિને હું નમસ્કાર કરું છું.

૨૩ **ૐ શ્રી યોગેશ્વરાય નમઃ** યોગના નિયંતા અથવા યોગના પ્રવર્તક એવા શ્રીહરિને હું નમસ્કાર કરું છું.

૨૪ **ૐ શ્રી યોગકલાપ્રવૃત્તયે નમઃ** યોગની અનેક પ્રકારની કલાઓને પ્રવર્તાવનારા એવાશ્રીહરિને હું વંદન કરું છું.

૨૫ **ૐ શ્રી અતિધૈર્યવતે નમઃ** અતિશય ધીરજતાથી યુકત એવા શ્રીહરિને હું નમસ્કાર કરું છું.

૨૬ **ૐ શ્રી જ્ઞાનિને નમઃ** સર્વેના મનના સંકલ્પને જાણનારા એવા પરમાત્માને હું નમસ્કાર કરું છું.
૨૭ **ૐ શ્રી પરમહંસાય નમઃ** અતિશય શુદ્ધ સ્વરૂપ પરમહંસ(સ્વરૂપ) એવા શ્રીહરિને હું નમસ્કાર કરું છું.
૨૮ **ૐ શ્રી તીર્થકૃતે નમઃ** સર્વે તીર્થોમાં વિચરણ કરનારા અથવા સર્વેને તીર્થરૂપ કરનારા એવા શ્રીહરિને હું નમસ્કાર કરું છું.
૨૯ **ૐ શ્રી તૈર્થિકાર્ચિતાય નમઃ** તીર્થમાં રહેનારા જનોએ જેમની પૂજા કરેલી છે એવા શ્રીહરિને હું નમસ્કાર કરું છું.
૩૦ **ૐ શ્રી ક્ષમાનિધયે નમઃ** ક્ષમાના સાગર એવા શ્રીહરિને હું નમસ્કાર કરું છું.
૩૧ **ૐ શ્રી સદોન્નિદ્રાય નમઃ** હમેશાં નિદ્રાથી રહિત એવા શ્રીહરિને હું નમસ્કાર કરું છું.
૩૨ **ૐ શ્રી ધ્યાનનિષ્ઠાય નમઃ** નિરંતર ધ્યાનમાં નિષ્ઠાવાળા એવા પરમાત્મા શ્રીહરિને હું નમસ્કાર કરું છું.
૩૩ **ૐ શ્રી તપઃપ્રિયાય નમઃ** તપ જેને પ્રિય છે એવા શ્રીહરિને હું નમસ્કાર કરું છું.
૩૪ **ૐ શ્રી સિદ્ધેશ્વરાય નમઃ** સર્વે સિદ્ધોના નિયંતા એવા શ્રીહરિને હું નમસ્કાર કરું છું.
૩૫ **ૐ શ્રી સ્વતન્ત્રાય નમઃ** સ્વતંત્ર એવા શ્રીહરિને હું નમસ્કાર કરું છું.
૩૬ **ૐ શ્રી બ્રહ્મવિધાપ્રવર્તકાય નમઃ** બ્રહ્મવિધાને પ્રવર્તાવનારા એવા શ્રીહરિને હું નમસ્કાર કરું છું.
૩૭ **ૐ શ્રી પાખંડોચ્છેદનપટવે નમઃ** પાખંડને ઉખેડી નાખવામાં કુશળ એવા શ્રીહરિને હું નમસ્કાર કરું છું.
૩૮ **ૐ શ્રી સ્વસ્વરૂપાચલસ્થિતયે નમઃ** પોતાના આત્મ સ્વરૂપને વિષે જ જેમની અચળ સ્થિતિ છે એવા પરમાત્મા શ્રીહરિને હું નમસ્કાર કરું છું.
૩૯ **ૐ શ્રી પ્રશાન્તમૂર્તયે નમઃ** કામક્રોધાદિક દોષથી રહિત અતિશય શાંત મૂર્તિ છે જેમની, એવા શ્રીહરિને હું નમસ્કાર કરું છું.
૪૦ **ૐ શ્રી નિર્દોષાય નમઃ** માયાના સર્વે દોષોથી રહિત એવા નિર્દોષ પરમાત્મા શ્રીહરિને હું નમસ્કાર કરું છું.
૪૧ **ૐ શ્રી અસુરગુર્વાદિમોહનાય નમઃ** આસુરી ગુરૂઓ તથા આસુરી રાજાઓને મોહ પમાડનારા એવા શ્રીહરિને હું નમસ્કાર કરું છું.
૪૨ **ૐ શ્રી અતિકારુણ્યનયનાય નમઃ** અતિશય કરૂણામય જેમનાં નેત્રો છે એવા શ્રીહરિને હું નમસ્કાર કરું છું.
૪૩ **ૐ શ્રી ઉદ્ધવાધ્વપ્રવર્તકાય નમઃ** ઉદ્ધવ સંપ્રદાયને પ્રવર્તાવનારા એવા શ્રીહરિને હું નમસ્કાર કરું છું.
૪૪ **ૐ શ્રી મહાવ્રતાયનમઃ** મહાવ્રતને ધારણ કરનારા એવા શ્રીહરિને હું નમસ્કાર કરું છું.
૪૫ **ૐ શ્રી સાધુશીલાય નમઃ** જેમનો સ્વભાવ અતિશય સરલ છે એવા પરમાત્માને હું નમસ્કાર કરું છું.
૪૬ **ૐ શ્રી સાધુવિપ્રપ્રપૂજકાય નમઃ** સાધુ અને બ્રાહ્મણોને પૂજનારા એવા શ્રીહરિને હું નમસ્કાર કરું છું.
૪૭ **ૐ શ્રી અહિંસયજ્ઞપ્રસ્તોત્રે નમઃ** અહિંસામય યજ્ઞની અતિશય પ્રશંસા કરનારા એવા શ્રીહરિને હું નમસ્કાર કરું છું.
૪૮ **ૐ શ્રી સાકારબ્રહ્મવર્ણનાય નમઃ** સાકાર બ્રહ્મનું વર્ણન કરનારા એવા પરમાત્મા શ્રીહરિને હું વંદન કરું છું.
૪૯ **ૐ શ્રી સ્વામિનારાયણ નમઃ** સર્વેના સ્વામી અને સર્વેના પ્રવર્તક એવા નારાયણરૂપ જે શ્રીહરિ તેને હું વંદન કરું છું.
૫૦ **ૐ શ્રી સ્વામિને નમઃ** સર્વેના નિયંતા એવા શ્રીહરિને હું વંદન કરું છું.
૫૧ **ૐ શ્રી કાલદોષનિવારકાય નમઃ** કળી કાળના દોષને નિવારણ કરનારા એવા શ્રીહરિને હું વંદન કરું છું.
૫૨ **ૐ શ્રી સચ્છાસ્ત્રવ્યસનાય નમઃ** સચ્છાસ્ત્રના અભ્યાસનું જેમને વ્યસન છે એવા શ્રીહરિને હું નમસ્કાર કરું છું.
૫૩ **ૐ શ્રી સધ્યઃસમાધિસ્થિતિકારકાય નમઃ** ભકતજનોને તત્કાળ જ સમાધિનિષ્ઠ બનાવનાર એવા શ્રીહરિને હું નમસ્કાર કરું છું.
૫૪ **ૐ શ્રી કૃષ્ણાર્ચાસ્થાયનકરાય નમઃ** કૃષ્ણની પૂજાને સ્થાપન કરનારા એવા શ્રીહરિને હું નમસ્કાર કરું છું.
૫૫ **ૐ શ્રી કૌલદ્વિષે નમઃ** કોલ મનનો દ્વેષ કરનારા એવા શ્રીહરિને હું નમસ્કાર કરું છું.

૫૬ **ૐ શ્રી કલિતારકાય નમઃ** ભકતોને કલિયુગથી તારનારા એવા શ્રીહરિને હું નમસ્કાર કરું છું.
૫૭ **ૐ શ્રી પ્રકાશરૂપાય નમઃ** અતિશય પ્રકાશમય જેમનું સ્વરૂપ છે એવા પરમાત્મા શ્રીહરિને હું નમસ્કાર કરું છું.
૫૮ **ૐ શ્રી નિર્દંભાય નમઃ** હમેશાં દંભથી રહિત એવા શ્રીહરિને હું નમસ્કાર કરું છું.
૫૯ **ૐ શ્રી સર્વજીવહિતાવહાય નમઃ** સર્વે જીવાત્માઓનું હમેશાં હિત કરનારા એવા શ્રીહરિને હું નમસ્કાર કરું છું.
૬૦ **ૐ શ્રી ભકિતસંપોષકાય નમઃ** ભકિતનું પોષણ કરનારા એવા શ્રીહરિને હું નમસ્કાર કરું છું.
૬૧ **ૐ શ્રી વાગ્મીને નમઃ** વાણી જેમની નિયમમાં છે એવા શ્રીહરિને હું વંદન કરું છું.
૬૨ **ૐ શ્રી ચતુર્વર્ગફલપ્રદાય નમઃ** ધર્મ, અર્થ, કામ અને મોક્ષ આ ચારેય પુરૂષાર્થને ફળના આપનારા એવા શ્રીહરિને હું નમસ્કાર કરું છું.
૬૩ **ૐ શ્રી નિર્મત્સરાય નમઃ** મત્સરથી રહિત એવા પરમાત્માને હું નમસ્કાર કરું છું.
૬૪ **ૐ શ્રી ભકતવર્મણે નમઃ** ભકતોનું રક્ષણ કરનારા કવચની સમાન એવા શ્રીહરિને હું વંદન કરું છું.
૬૫ **ૐ શ્રી બુધ્ધિદાત્રે નમઃ** સર્વે જનોને બુદ્ધિ આપનારા એવા શ્રીહરિને હું નમસ્કાર કરું છું.
૬૬ **ૐ શ્રી અતિપાવનાય નમઃ** અતિ પવિત્ર સ્વરૂપ પરમાત્માને હું નમસ્કાર કરું છું.
૬૭ **ૐ શ્રી અબુદ્ધિહૃતે નમઃ** દૂષ્ટ બુદ્ધિનું હરણ કરનારા એવા શ્રીહરિને હું નમસ્કાર કરું છું.
૬૮ **ૐ શ્રી બ્રહ્મધામદર્શકાય નમઃ** બ્રહ્મધામને બતાવનારા એવા શ્રીહરિને હું વંદન કરું છું.
૬૯ **ૐ શ્રી અપરાજીતાય નમઃ** કોઇનાથી પણ પરાજ્યને નહિં પામેલા એવા શ્રીહરિને હું નમસ્કાર કરું છું.
૭૦ **ૐ શ્રી આસમુદ્રાન્તસત્કીર્તયે નમઃ** સમુદ્ર પર્યન્ત વિસ્તરેલી છે સત્કીર્તિ જેમની એવા શ્રીહરિને હું નમસ્કાર કરું છું.
૭૧ **ૐ શ્રી શ્રિતસંસૃતિમોચનાય નમઃ** પોતાના આશ્રિતોને જન્મ મરણરૂપી સંસૃતિ થકી મૂકાવનારા એવા શ્રીહરિને હું નમસ્કાર કરું છું.
૭૨ **ૐ શ્રી ઉદારાય નમઃ** જનોને દાન આપવામાં ઉદાર એવા શ્રીહરિને હું નમસ્કાર કરું છું.
૭૩ **ૐ શ્રી સહજાનંદાય નમઃ** સ્વભાવસિદ્ધ જ જેમને આનંદ રહેલો છે એવા પરમાત્મા શ્રીહરિને હું નમસ્કાર કરું છું.
૭૪ **ૐ શ્રી સાધ્વીધર્મપ્રવર્તકાય નમઃ** એકાન્તિક પતિવ્રતાના ધર્મને પ્રવર્તાવનારા એવા શ્રીહરિને હું નમસ્કાર કરું છું.
૭૫ **ૐ શ્રી કંદર્પદર્પદલનાય નમઃ** કામદેવના ગર્વને હણી નાખનારા એવા શ્રીહરિને હું નમસ્કાર કરું છું.
૭૬ **ૐ શ્રી વૈષ્ણવક્રતુકારકાય નમઃ** વિષ્ણુ સંબંધી યજ્ઞને પ્રવર્તાવનારા એવા શ્રીહરિને વંદન કરુંછું.
૭૭ **ૐ શ્રી પંચાયતનસન્માનાય નમઃ** વિષ્ણુ, શિવ, ગણપતિ, પાર્વતી અને સૂર્ય આ પાંચ દેવોનું સન્માન કરનારા એવા શ્રીહરિને હું નમસ્કાર કરું છું.
૭૮ **ૐ શ્રી નૈષ્ઠિકવ્રતપોષકાય નમઃ** નૈષ્ઠિકબ્રહ્મચર્યવ્રતનું પોષણ કરનારા એવા શ્રીહરિને હું નમસ્કાર કરું છું.
૭૯ **ૐ શ્રી પ્રગલ્ભાય નમઃ** સર્વે જનોને રંજન કરનારા ચતુર એવા શ્રીહરિને હું નમસ્કાર કરું છું.
૮૦ **ૐ શ્રી નિઃસ્પૃહાય નમઃ** વિષયોને વિષે સ્પૃહાથી રહિત એવા પરમાત્માને હું નમસ્કાર કરું છું.
૮૧ **ૐ શ્રી સત્યપ્રતિજ્ઞાય નમઃ** સત્ય છે પ્રતિજ્ઞા જેમની એવા પરમાત્મા શ્રીહરિને હું નમસ્કાર કરું છું.
૮૨ **ૐ શ્રી ભકતવત્સલાય નમઃ** ભકતજનો ઉપર વહાલ રાખનારા એવા શ્રીહરિને હું વંદન કરું છું.
૮૩ **ૐ શ્રી અરોષણાય નમઃ** હમેશા ક્રોધથી રહિત એવા શ્રીહરિને હું વંદન કરું છું.
૮૪ **ૐ શ્રી દીર્ઘદર્શિને નમઃ** વિશાળ જેમની દૃષ્ટિ છે એવા પરમાત્માને હું નમસ્કાર કરું છું.
૮૫ **ૐ શ્રી ષડૂર્મિવિજ્યક્ષમાય નમઃ** ભૂખ અને તરસ, માન અને અપમાન, સુખ અને દુઃખ આ છ ઉર્મીઓ ઉપર વિજય મેળવવામાં સમર્થ એવા શ્રીહરિને હું નમસ્કાર કરું છું.
૮૬ **ૐ શ્રી નિરહંકૃતયે નમઃ** અહંકારથી રહિત એવા શ્રીહરિને હું નમસ્કાર કરું છું.
૮૭ **ૐ શ્રી અદ્રોહાય નમઃ** કોઇનો પણ દ્રોહ નહિ કરનારા એવા પરમાત્મા શ્રીહરિને હું નમસ્કાર કરું છું.
૮૮ **ૐ શ્રી ઋજવે નમઃ** સરળ સ્વભાવવાળા એવા પરમાત્માને હું વંદન કરું છું.

૮૯ **ૐ શ્રી સર્વોપકારકાય નમઃ** સર્વે જનો ઉપર ઉપકારને કરનારા એવા પરમાત્માને હું નમસ્કાર કરું છું.
૯૦ **ૐ શ્રી નિયામકાય નમઃ** સર્વે જીવો અને ઇશ્વરોના નિયામક એવા શ્રીહરિને હું વંદન કરું છું.
૯૧ **ૐ શ્રી ઉપશમસ્થિતયે નમઃ** હમેશાં દેહની સ્મૃતિથી રહિત એવી ઉપશમ અવસ્થામાં રહેનારા એવા શ્રીહરિને હું નમસ્કાર કરું છું.
૯૨ **ૐ શ્રી વિનયવતે નમઃ** વિનયથી યુકત એવા શ્રીહરિને હું નમસ્કાર કરું છું.
૯૩ **ૐ શ્રી ગુરવે નમઃ** સર્વેના ગુરૂ એવા શ્રીહરિને હું વંદન કરું છું.
૯૪ **ૐ શ્રી અજાતવૈરિણે નમઃ** જેમનો કોઇ શત્રુ પણ જન્મેલો નથી એવા શ્રીહરિને હું નમસ્કાર કરું છું.
૯૫ **ૐ શ્રી નિર્લોભાય નમઃ** હમેશાં લોભથી રહિત એવા શ્રીહરિને હું નમસ્કાર કરું છું.
૯૬ **ૐ શ્રી મહાપુરૂષાય નમઃ** સર્વે પુરૂષો કરતાં મહાન એવા શ્રીહરિને હું નમસ્કાર કરું છું.
૯૭ **ૐ શ્રી આત્મદાય નમઃ** ભકતોને પોતાની મૂર્તિ આપી દેનારા એવા શ્રીહરિને હું નમસ્કાર કરુંછું.
૯૮ **ૐ શ્રી અખંડિતાર્ષમર્યાદાય નમઃ** ધર્મમર્યાદાનું કયારે પણ ખંડન નહિં કરનારા એવા શ્રીહરિને હું નમસ્કાર કરું છું.
૯૯ **ૐ શ્રી વ્યાસસિદ્ધાન્તબોધકાય નમઃ** વ્યાસના સિદ્ધાન્તને જણાવનારા એવા શ્રીહરિને હું નમસ્કાર કરું છું.
૧૦૦ **ૐ શ્રી મનોનિગ્રહયુકિતજ્ઞાય નમઃ** મનના નિગ્રહની યુકિતને જાણનારા એવા શ્રીહરિને હું નમસ્કાર કરું છું.
૧૦૧ **ૐ શ્રી યમદૂતવિમોચકાય નમઃ** યમદૂત થકી મૂકાવનારા એવા શ્રીહરિને હું વંદન કરું છું.
૧૦૨ **ૐ શ્રી પૂર્ણકામાય નમઃ** જેમના મનોરથો પૂર્ણ થયેલા છે એવા શ્રીહરિને હું વંદન કરું છું.
૧૦૩ **ૐ શ્રી સત્યવાદિને નમઃ** હમેશાં સત્ય બોલનારા એવા શ્રીહરિને હું વંદન કરું છું.
૧૦૪ **ૐ શ્રી ગુણગ્રાહિણે નમઃ** હમેશાં ગુણોને જ ગ્રહણ કરનારા એવા શ્રીહરિને હું નમસ્કાર કરું છું.
૧૦૫ **ૐ શ્રી ગતસ્મયાય નમઃ** ગર્વથી રહિત એવા શ્રીહરિને હું નમસ્કાર કરું છું.
૧૦૬ **ૐ શ્રી સદાચારપ્રિયતરાય નમઃ** સદાચાર જેમને અતિશય પ્રિય છે એવા શ્રીહરિને હું નમસ્કાર કરું છું.
૧૦૭ **ૐ શ્રી પુણ્યશ્રવણકીર્તનાય નમઃ** પુણ્યને આપનારૂં છે શ્રવણ અને કીર્તન જેમનું એવા શ્રીહરિને હું નમસ્કાર કરું છું.
૧૦૮ **ૐ શ્રી સર્વમંગલસદ્રૂપનાનાગુણવિચેષ્ટિતાય નમઃ** જેમનું સ્વરૂપ, જેમના ચરિત્રો સર્વને મંગળ કરનારાં છે એવા શ્રીહરિને હું નમસ્કાર કરું છું.

॥ ઇતિ જનમંગલનામાવલી સમાપ્તા ॥

Swaminarayan Temples in the UK

Shree Swaminarayan Temple Oldham
270 Lee Street, Oldham, Lancashire OL8 1BG
Tel/ Fax: 0161 652 0993

Shree Swaminarayan Temple Willesden
220-222 Willesden Lane, Willesden, London NW2 5RG
Tel: 0208 459 3084

SKS Swaminarayan Temple Bolton
1-11 Adelaide Street, Bolton BL3 3NT
Tel: 01204 652 604

Shree Swaminarayan Temple Cardiff
4 Merches Place, Grange Town, Cardiff CF1 7RD
Tel: 02920 371 128

SKS Swaminarayan Temple Woolwich
St Margaret Grove, Plumstead Common, London SE18 7RL
Tel: 0208 854 0823

SKS Swaminarayan Temple East London
22-24 Shaftesbury Road, Forest Gate, London E7 8PZ
Tel: 0208 470 9375

SKS Swaminarayan Temple Harrow
Westfield Lane, Kenton, Harrow HA3 9EA
Tel: 0208 909 9899

Shree Swaminarayan Temple Leicester (ISSO)
139-141 Loughborough Road, Leicester LE4 5LQ
Tel: 0116 266 6210

Shree Swaminarayan Temple Croydon (ISSO)
72 Colmer Road, Streatham, London SW16 5JE
Tel: 0208 679 8050

Shree Swaminarayan Temple Brighton (ISSO)
79A Trafalgar Road, Portslade, Brighton BN41 1XD
Tel: 01273 420 200

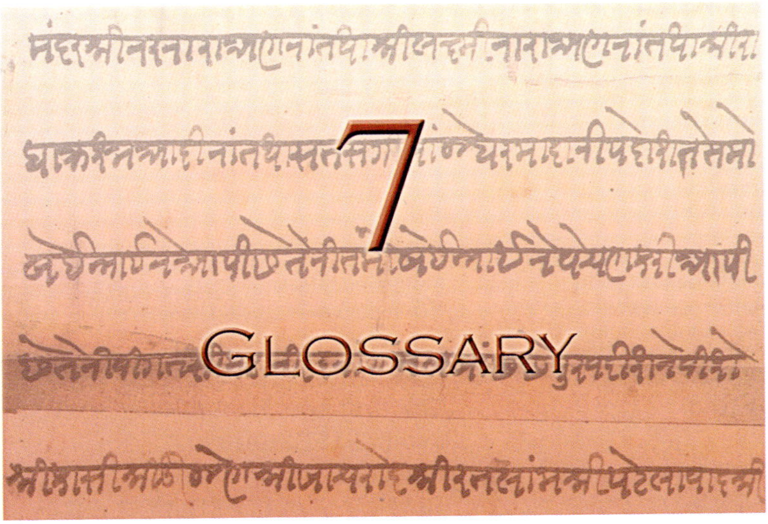

Aantar Atma	Inner soul
Aarti	Prayer offered to God with lamps
Achaman	Act involving sipping of water three times to purify the soul
Acharya	Head of sampraday, spiritual leader
Adharma	Unrighteous way of life
Aditya	Sun God
Agni Dev	God of Fire
Ahavan mantra	Mantra used to invite Lord to reside in the murti
Ahankar	Action resulting from the Mana, Buddhi and Chita process
Ahimsa	Non violence, non killing and respect for living beings
Ahmedabad	Centre of NarNarayan Dev diocese
Akshardham	Divine heaven of Lord Swaminarayan
Amrut	Divine nectar
Ankoot	Large variety of food offered to God

Anaj	Foodstuffs including pulses, grain, corn, etc.
Aradhna	Devotional effort
Arjun	Third of the Pandav brothers, famousarcher
Artha	Wealth
Ashram	A stage of life, place where devotees live
Astanga	Form of yoga
Atharva-Veda	Fourth Vedas, deals with knowledge of science
Atma	Soul
Aum	The first sound from God, sacred symbol of Hinduism
Avatar	Incarnations of God
Ayodhya	Birthplace of Lord Ram
Ayodhyaprasad	First Acharya of the Ahmedabad diocese, appointed by Lord Swaminarayan
Ayurveda	Ancient form of medicine
Badrikashram	Divine heaven of Lord NarNarayan
Bala Krishna	Father of Dharmadev
Baldev	Brother of Lord Krishna
Bhaguji	Personal servant of Lord Swaminarayan
Bhagyawati	Mother of Dharmadev
Bhajans	Devotional songs of God
Bhakta	Devotee of God
Bhakti	Devotion
Bhaktimata	Mother of Lord Swaminarayan
Bharat	Brother of Lord Ram
Bharatkhund	Indian sub continent
Bhawani Devi	Mother of Bhaktimata
Brahm	Soul that has escaped from the cycle of birth and death
Brahma	Creator, one of the Trimurti
Brahmand	Universe
Brahmapur	Divine heaven of God
Brahmchari	Celibate

Brahmin	Highest Hindu caste
Buddha	Incarnation of Lord Vishnu
Buddhi	Knowledge stored in the mind from previous experience
Chakra	Weapon held by Lord Vishnu
Chandlo	The red circular dot made on the forehead of kumkum
Chhapaiya	Birthplace of Lord Swaminarayan
Cheen	Divine signs on the feet of Lord Swaminarayan
Chiranjeeva	One who has a long life
Chita	Sub-conscious mind questioning the initial thought
Dadakhachar	King of Gadhada, great devotee of Lord Swaminarayan
Dakshin Desh	Southern region
Dandvat	Method of darshan for males
Darshan	Visualisation of God
Dasaratha	Father of Lord Ram
Dharma	Righteous way of life
Dharmadev	Father of Lord Swaminarayan
Dharmakul	Family of Dharmadev
Dhyan	Meditation
Diksha	Initiation into religious fellowship
Dvija	Twice born
Dwaparyug	Third age
Ekadashi	Day of fast and penance, falling on the eleventh day of each lunar cycle
Gadhada	Divine centre of sampraday during life of Lord Swaminarayan
Ganesh	Son of Shiva, deity with an elephant head, remover of obstacles
Ganga	Sacred river of India
Gangaba	Devout follower of Lord Swaminarayan from Jetalpur
Garudji	Divine transport of Lord Vishnu
Gaumukhi	Pouch for mala

Ghanshyam	Childhood name of Lord Swaminarayan
Gnan	Knowledge
Goloka	Divine heaven of Lord Krishna
Gopinath Dev	Image of God installed at Gadhada by Lord Swaminarayan
Gopis	Devotees of Lord Krishna
Grahastha	Second stage of Hindu life, entered into after marriage, householder
Guna	Form of quality
Guru	Spiritual teacher
Hanuman	Devout servant of Lord Ram, in the form of a monkey
Hari	One of the four names given to Lord Swaminarayan by Markendey Muni
Haridas	Servant of God
Harigita	Knowledge given to Bhaktimata at time of passing away by Ghanshyam
HariKrishna	One of the four names given to Lord Swaminarayan by Markendey Muni
Hariprasad	Dharmadev
Havan	Act of worship where ghee and grains are offered into fire
Hindola	Swing of God
Iccharamji	Younger brother of Lord Swaminarayan
Indrajit	Son of Ravana
Indriya	Sense
Ishwar	God
Jaap	Form of worship involving the repetition of a mantra
Janaka	Father of Sita
Janmashtami	Birthday of Lord Krishna
Janoi	Sacred thread
Jatanba	Devout follower of Lord Swaminarayan from Dhangarva

Jeeva	Soul
Jinabhai	Devout follower of Lord Swaminarayan, King of Panchala
Jivuba	Devout follower of Lord Swaminarayan, sister of Dadakhachar
Kalidatta	Demon, who attempted to kill Ghanshyam at the age of three
Kaliyug	Fourth and current age
Kalki	Final incarnation of God
Kama	Pursuit of sexual desire
Kanthi	Double stranded tulsi necklace worn by all satsangis around the neck
Karma	Action
Kauravas	Sons of King Dhutrasta
Kirtan	Devotional song of God
Krishna	Incarnation of Vishnu
Krishna Sharma	Father of Bhaktimata
Krodh	Anger
Kshatriya	Warrior caste, second Hindu caste
Ladhiba	Devout follower of Lord Swaminarayan from Bhuj
Laduba	Devout follower of Lord Swaminarayan, sister of Dadakhachar
Laxman	Brother of Lord Ram
Laxmi	Goddess of wealth, consort of Lord Vishnu
LaxmiNarayan Dev	Image of God installed at Vadtal by Lord Swaminarayan
Leela	Divine story of God
Lingas	Stone symbol of Lord Shiva
Lobh	Greed
Madan Mohan Dev	Image of God installed at Dholera by Lord Swaminarayan
Maha Pooja	Grand worship of God
Mahabharat	Epic involving Lord Krishna
Mahadev	Lord Shiva

Mala	108 beaded thread used for reciting the name of God
Mana	Initiates the thought in the mind
Manaki	Divine horse of Lord Swaminarayan
Machabhakta	Follower of Lord Swaminarayan, King Khatwang of Kariyani
Mandir	Temple
Mantra	Sacred phrase
Mayaram Bhatt	Personal messenger of Lord Swaminarayan
Markendey Muni	The great astrologer who gave Lord Swaminarayan four names
Mathura	Birthplace of Lord Krishna
Manu Rishi	First law giver to mankind
Maya	God's power of attachment and desire
Moha	Emotional attachment
Moksha	Salvation
Murdanav	Demon, son of Nadijung
Murti	Image of God
Nar Narayan	Incarnation of Vishnu, Image of God installed at Ahmedabad and Bhuj by Lord Swaminarayan
Naradji	Son of Brahma, devotee of God
Narak	Hell
Nilkanth Varni	One of the four names given to Lord Swaminarayan by Markendey Muni. Name adopted by Almighty God Supreme whilst on pilgrimage.
Nitya Niyam	Daily recital of prayers
Paap	Sin
Panchvartman	Five vows for all satsangis
Pandavas	Five sons of King Pandu
Parbrahm	Almighty God Supreme
Parshuram	Incarnation of Lord Vishnu
Parvati	Consort of Lord Shiva
Pativrata	Ideal wife to whom her husband is God

Pavanputra	Hanuman
Patotsav	Anniversary of temples
Pooja	Worship of God
Prahalada	Son of Hiranyakashipu, nephew of Holika
Pralaya	End of the Universe
Prasad	Blessed offering of food
Pratakshya	In person
Pradikshana	Worship by walking around God in a clockwise direction
Punya	Benefit of good deed
Puran	Sanskrit scriptures
Purushottam	God
Pustak	Religious book
Raas	Devotional dance
Radha	Beloved consort of Lord Krishna
Radha Raman	*Dev* Image of God installed at Junagadh by Lord Swaminarayan
Raghuvirji	First Acharya of the Vadtal diocese, appointed by Lord Swaminarayan
Ram	Incarnation of Vishnu
Ramanand Swami	Guru of Lord Swaminarayan, incarnation of Uddhavji
Ramanuj Acharya	Guru of Ramanand Swami, incarnation of Laxman
Ramayan	Epic involving Lord Ram
Ramnavmi	Birthday of Lord Swaminarayan and Lord Ram
Rampratapji	Elder brother of Lord Swaminarayan
Ranchodrai	Image of God installed at Vadtal by Lord Swaminarayan
Ravana	Demon who kidnapped Sita
Rishi	Sage
Rug-Veda	First Vedas, deal with general knowledge
Sadhu	Saint, renoucer of material world
Samadhi	State of heavenly trance
Sampraday	Congregation, religious fellowship

Sam-Veda	Third Vedas, deals with knowledge of worship
Sangeet	Music
Sanskrit	Ancient language, in which scriptures are written, mother of all languages
Sakar	Existence in physical form
Sarovar	Large lake
Shikharbandh Temple	Temple where complete duties are performed on idols of God
Sanyasi	One who has entered the fourth stage of life
Saryudas	Lord Swaminarayan
Sarvaria Brahmin	Caste into which Lord Swaminarayan was born
Satyayug	First age
Seva	To help others without gain
Shankar	Lord Shiva
Sharad Poonam	Brightest full moon of the year
Shastras	Holy scriptures
Shatrughna	Brother of Lord Ram
Shaligram	Lord Vishnu in the form of a stone
Shikshapatri	Letter of teachings written by Lord Swaminarayan
Shiva	The destroyer God, one of the Trimurti
Shreemad Bhagwad Gita	Divine words of Lord Krishna to Arjun in Mahabharat
Shreemad Satsangi Jeevan	Life story of Lord Swaminarayan, written by Shatanand Swami
Shudra	Servant caste
Sugreeva	Brother of Vali, friend of Lord Ram, King of Kishkindha
Sumitra	Wife of King Dasaratha, mother of Laxman and Shatrughna
Sundarji Suthar	Devout follower of Lord Swaminarayan, advisor to the King of Bhuj, brother of Narayanji Suthar

Sura Khachar	Devout follower and friend of Lord Swaminarayan, King of Loya, possessing jovial characteristics
Suryanarayan	Sun God
Sutak	Days of impurity
Suvasinibai	Wife of Rampratapji
Swaminarayan	Almighty God Supreme, one mantra comprising of six syllables.
Tapa	Penance
Tirtha	Holy place
Tretayug	Second age
Trimurti	Trinity; Brahma, Vishnu and Shiva.
Triveni Sangam	Point where the Rivers Ganges, Yamuna and Saraswati meet in Prayagraj, Allahabad
Uddhav Sampraday	Original name for Swaminarayan sampraday
Uddhavji	Advisor of Lord Krishna
Urdhvarekha	The creases on Lord Swaminarayan's divine Lotus Feet
Urdhvapundra tilak	The U shaped mark made on the forehead with chandan
Vaayu	Wind God
Vachnamrit	Scripture, containing the divine spoken words of Lord Swaminarayan
Vadtal	Centre of LaxmiNarayan Dev diocese
Vaishiyas	Merchant and trader caste
Valmiki	Wrote the Ramayan, known as the first poet
Van Vicharan	Pilgrimage of Nilkanth Varni, His journey through forest
Vasant Panchmi	Day on which Lord Swaminarayan wrote the Shikshapatri
Vedas	Ancient Scriptures which are the foundations for Hinduism

Vibhishan	Brother of Ravana, devotee of Lord Ram
Visarjan Mantra	Mantra used to return Lord to His heavenly abode
Vishnu	The Preserver God, part of the Trimurti
Vishvamitra	First Kshatriya, became Rishi through observing penance
Visishtadwait	Philosophy of Ramanuj Acharya accepted by Lord Swaminarayan
Vikram Samvat (VS)	Counting of the Hindu calendar years commenced from his birth
Vivek	Respect
Vrata	Penance through control of diet
Vyas Muni	Incarnation of Vishnu, son of Parasar Rishi, author of Puran scriptures
Yagna	Sacred ceremony
Yajur-Veda	Second Vedas, deals with knowledge of karma
Yampuri	Hell, residence of Dharmaraj
Yug	Era

INDEX

A

B

G

H

I

N

O

P

R

S

T

U

V

W

Y

Z

Gratitude

We express our gratitude to all the sponsors of this publication. With their generosity we have been able to bring this book to print.

Jai Swaminarayan

Shree Swaminarayan Temple Oldham

Prime Sponsors

Aqualite Trading Ltd
Kings Kitchens Ltd

Major Sponsors

MHB Autospares
Patels Chemist
PBL Jewellers Ltd
Kenton Timber / City Deco
H&P Double Glazing Ltd
HSB Haughton Ltd
Saloria Printers
K D Developments
Laxmanbhai Group of Companies
Platt Lane Newsagents
Princes Video
Meera Catering
Elmpride Ltd
Parbat Shivji Kerai
Late V M Patel
Ashton Sweet Mart
Shivji Karsan Kerai

Minor Sponsors

Ajvani Shoes
All Bees Ltd
Amazing Tiles
Ashcon Ltd *(Building Contractor)*
Babla Pan Centre
Bani Associates Ltd
Barclays Bank Plc
Bharti Auto Spares
DD Insurance & Financial Services
DBF Associates
Durga Timber Europe Ltd
Euro-Par Interiors
First Manchester
Fourways Supplies
Gami Associates Ltd
Global Travels (Eccles)
Harish Kalyan Virji Vekaria
J Fox Sox Ltd
Jitendra Bhimji Devraj Kara
K & K Builders Ltd
Kalyan Khimji Karsan Garara
Kantilal Velji Bhudia
Karsons Photographers
KBMD Registered Auditors
Kenford Builders

Minor Sponsors

Kutch Engineering Works
M.N.Autos Ltd
Malbro Construction
Manji Karsan Gangjiani & Sons
Manji Kurji Lalji Raghwani
Mina World Travel Services
Modern Upholstery
Office Express
Om Video
Patel & Co.
Patel Architects
Pravin Murji Jadva Vekariya
Premiere Eurocom
Premji Harji Devji Gorasia & Sons
Lalji Dhanji Jesani
Premji Velji Naran Vekaria
Prizma Windows Ltd
Ravji Dhanji Kerai
Late Ratna Vasta Thakerani
Sonalink Ltd
Stanton Group
Super Glazed Ltd
Surge-IT Ltd
Surya Restaurant
Valji Devshi Lalji Rabadia
Vinod Shivji Kerai
Vishram Hirji Bhudia
Washington Windows

Complimentary Sponsors

A R & S A News
Anita Traders
Govind Kanji Raghvani
Govind Premji Thakarani
Govind Ramji Bhudia
H D Gami
Harish Kanji Pindoria
Hirji Arjan Hirani
Hirji Harji Varsani
Jayan Pravin Shamji Varsani
Jayesh Naran Sojitra
Manji Harji Gorasia
Manji Jina Hirani
Nanji Meghji Hirani
Naran Devji Hirani
Naran Parbat Sojitra
Nathalal Karsan Halai
Premji Gopal Bhudia
Late Radhabai Premji Valji Varsani
Ramji Harji Bhudia
Rohan Naresh Varsani
Sheila Kurji Bhimji Kerai
Shivan Harish Shamji Varsani
Shivji Karshan Jeshani
Valji Devji Khimji Raghwani
Valji Ramji Jadva Vekria
Vascroft Contractors Ltd